PEARSON

my Student JOURNAL

This Student Journal belongs to

____

PEARSON

Boston, Massachusetts
Chandler, Arizona
Glenview, Illinois
Upper Saddle River, New Jersey

Acknowledgments appear on page 234, which constitute an extension of this copyright page.

ISBN-13:   978-0-13-363803-5
ISBN-10:   0-13-363803-0
11 12 13 14 V011 19 18 17 16 15

How to Use This Book

The *myWorld Geography Student Journal* is a tool to help you process and record what you have learned from the Student Edition of *myWorld Geography*. As you complete the activities and essays in your Journal, you will be creating your own personal resource for reviewing the concepts, key terms, and maps from *myWorld Geography*. The Journal worksheets and writing exercises focus on the Essential Question, helping you uncover the relevance of each chapter to your life.

The **Essential Question Preview** will help you understand the chapter you are about to read. Begin with Connect to Your Life to find ways to relate the issues and principles of the Essential Questions to your life—your family, school, or community. Next, Connect to the Chapter invites you to flip through the chapter and chart your predictions on how the Essential Question relates to the countries in each chapter.

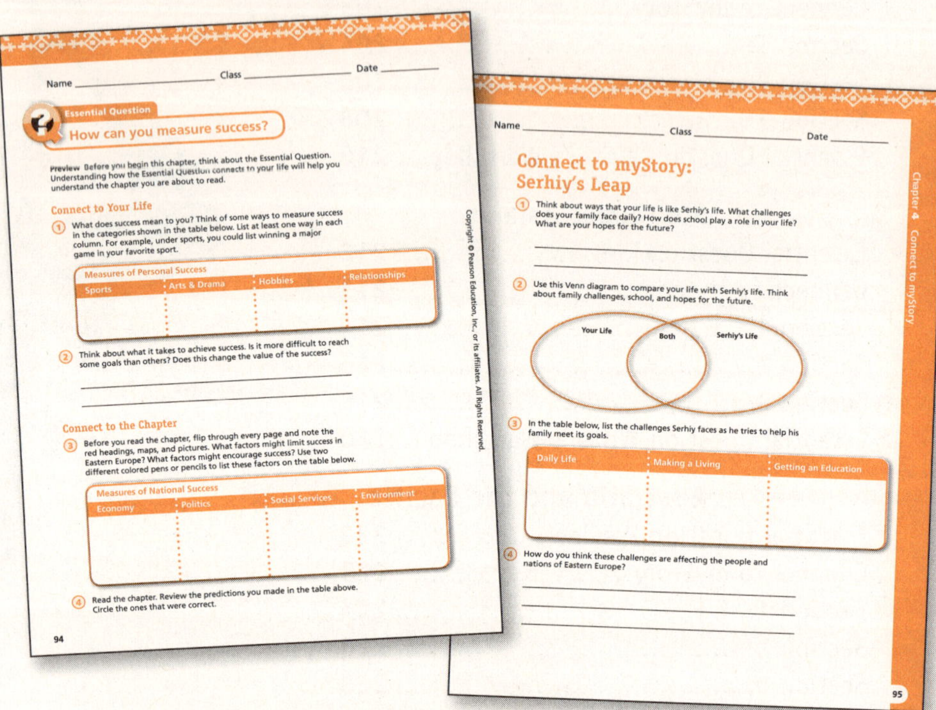

You will build your Map Skills and make the maps your own by locating features on the line maps in **Take Notes.** You can synthesize concepts and create a detailed visual study guide by filling in the illustrated graphic organizers in Take Notes. Each Take Notes page ends with an exercise that helps you draw conclusions about the Essential Question.

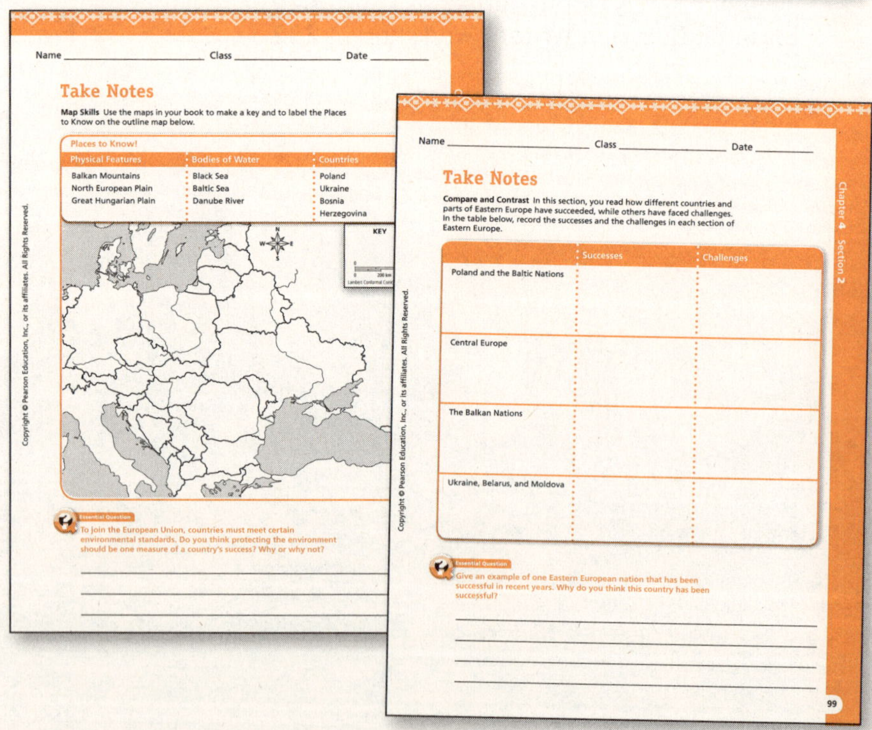

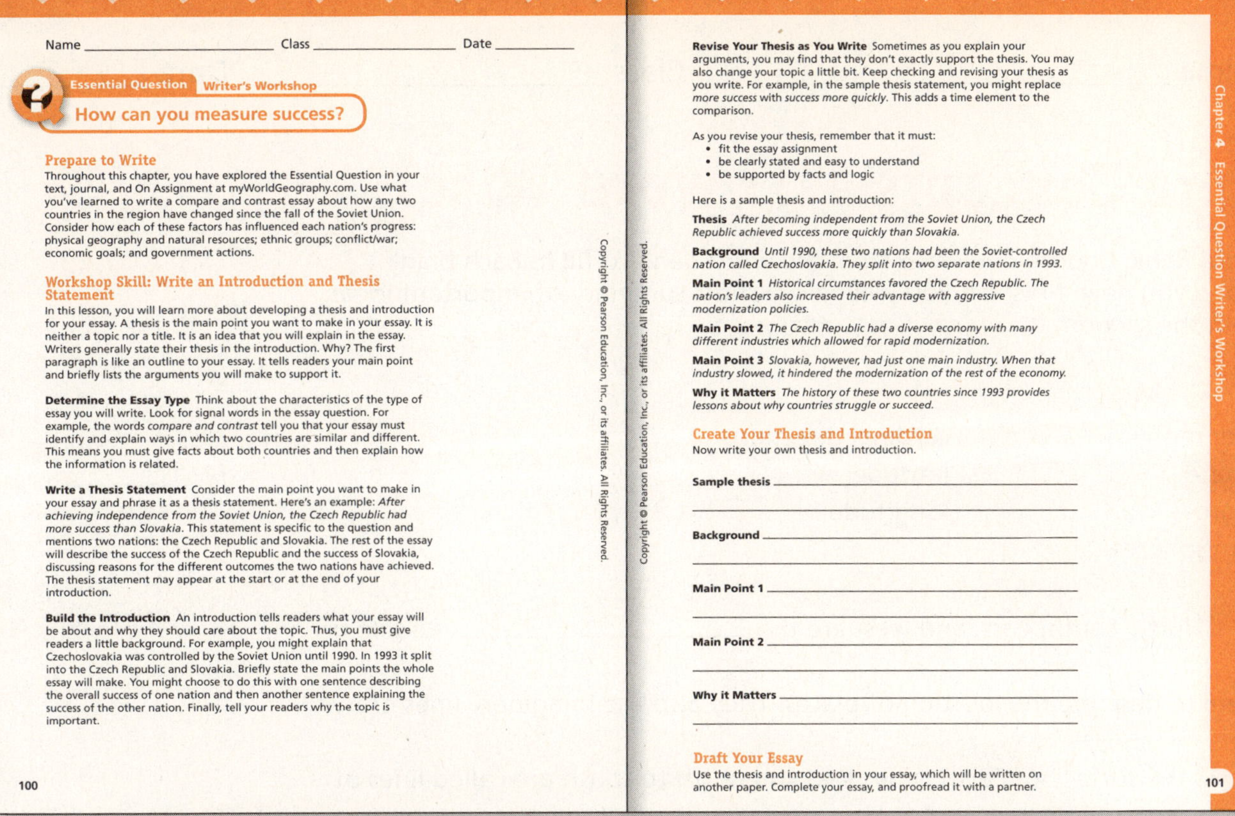

Name ___________________ Class ___________ Date __________

Essential Question Writer's Workshop
How can you measure success?

Prepare to Write
Throughout this chapter, you have explored the Essential Question in your text, journal, and On Assignment at myWorldGeography.com. Use what you've learned to write a compare and contrast essay about how any two countries in the region have changed since the fall of the Soviet Union. Consider how each of these factors has influenced each nation's progress: physical geography and natural resources; ethnic groups; conflict/war; economic goals; and government actions.

Workshop Skill: Write an Introduction and Thesis Statement
In this lesson, you will learn more about developing a thesis and introduction for your essay. A thesis is the main point you want to make in your essay. It is neither a topic nor a title. It is an idea that you will explain in the essay. Writers generally state their thesis in the introduction. Why? The first paragraph is like an outline to your essay. It tells readers your main point and briefly lists the arguments you will make to support it.

Determine the Essay Type Think about the characteristics of the type of essay you will write. Look for signal words in the essay question. For example, the words *compare and contrast* tell you that your essay must identify and explain ways in which two countries are similar and different. This means you must give facts about both countries and then explain how the information is related.

Write a Thesis Statement Consider the main point you want to make in your essay and phrase it as a thesis statement. Here's an example: *After achieving independence from the Soviet Union, the Czech Republic had more success than Slovakia.* This statement is specific to the question and mentions two nations: the Czech Republic and Slovakia. The rest of the essay will describe the success of the Czech Republic and the success of Slovakia, discussing reasons for the different outcomes the two nations have achieved. The thesis statement may appear at the start or at the end of your introduction.

Build the Introduction An introduction tells readers what your essay will be about and why they should care about the topic. Thus, you must give readers a little background. For example, you might explain that Czechoslovakia was controlled by the Soviet Union until 1990. In 1993 it split into the Czech Republic and Slovakia. Briefly state the main points the whole essay will make. You might choose to do this with one sentence describing the overall success of one nation and then another sentence explaining the success of the other nation. Finally, tell your readers why the topic is important.

Revise Your Thesis as You Write Sometimes as you explain your arguments, you may find that they don't exactly support the thesis. You may also change your topic a little bit. Keep checking and revising your thesis as you write. For example, in the sample thesis statement, you might replace *more success* with *success more quickly*. This adds a time element to the comparison.

As you revise your thesis, remember that it must:
- fit the essay assignment
- be clearly stated and easy to understand
- be supported by facts and logic

Here is a sample thesis and introduction:

Thesis *After becoming independent from the Soviet Union, the Czech Republic achieved success more quickly than Slovakia.*

Background *Until 1990, these two nations had been the Soviet-controlled nation called Czechoslovakia. They split into two separate nations in 1993.*

Main Point 1 *Historical circumstances favored the Czech Republic. The nation's leaders also increased their advantage with aggressive modernization policies.*

Main Point 2 *The Czech Republic had a diverse economy with many different industries which allowed for rapid modernization.*

Main Point 3 *Slovakia, however, had just one main industry. When that industry slowed, it hindered the modernization of the rest of the economy.*

Why it Matters *The history of these two countries since 1993 provides lessons about why countries struggle or succeed.*

Create Your Thesis and Introduction
Now write your own thesis and introduction.

Sample thesis ___________________________________

Background ___________________________________

Main Point 1 ___________________________________

Main Point 2 ___________________________________

Why it Matters ___________________________________

Draft Your Essay
Use the thesis and introduction in your essay, which will be written on another paper. Complete your essay, and proofread it with a partner.

Chapter 4 Essential Question Writer's Workshop

100   101

The **Essential Question Writer's Workshop** provides you an end-of-chapter opportunity to show your understanding of chapter content by writing about the Essential Question. Each Workshop features instruction and practice with one of the skills you will need to write an essay and express your ideas. The Writer's Workshop exercises and the activities you have completed in your Journal will help you draw conclusions about the Chapter Essential Question.

The **Word Wise** exercises give you the chance to really get to know and explore the key terms through word maps, crossword puzzles, and other game formats.

Name _______________ Class _______________ Date _______

Word Wise
Crossword Puzzle The clues describe key terms from this section. Fill in the numbered Across boxes with the correct key terms. Then, do the same with the Down clues.

Across
1. a Muslim house of worship
2. a culture that has writing and where people do many different types of jobs
3. a group with less than half of the population

Down
4. worshipping only one god
5. the holy book of Islam
6. an all-powerful leader who has complete control over a nation
7. an Islamic political and religious leader

146

Name ___________________ Class ___________ Date _________

Word Wise
Vocabulary Quiz Show Some quiz shows ask a question and expect the contestant to give the answer. In other shows, the contestant is given an answer and must supply the question. If the blank is in the question column, write the question that would result in the answer given. If the question is supplied, write the appropriate answer.

QUESTION
1. What do you call a person who sets up and manages his or her own business?
2. _______________
3. If one part of a country breaks away from that country and declares itself a new nation, what is that action called?
4. _______________
5. What is the word for a specific style of food?

ANSWER
1. _______________
2. ethnic cleansing
3. _______________
4. capital
5. _______________

98

Core Concepts 1.1: Word Wise

Word Bank Choose one word from the word bank to fill in each blank.
When you have finished, you will have a short summary of important ideas
from the section.

Word Bank

geography	cardinal directions
sphere	latitude
degrees	longitude
hemispheres	

North, south, east, and west are the _____________________. People use

them to describe the location of places. They also use imaginary lines drawn

across the surface of Earth. Lines that run north to south are called lines of

_____________________, while those that run east to west are lines of

_____________________. These lines are measured in units called

_____________________. Each one of these lines goes in a circle around Earth,

which has the shape of a _____________________. The equator is the east-

west line that runs across the center of Earth. The equator divides our planet

into two equal _____________________, or halves. The study of Earth and its

human and non-human features is called _____________________.

Name _________________________ Class _________________________ Date ____________

Core Concepts 1.2: Word Wise

Words In Context For each question below, write an answer that shows your understanding of the boldfaced key term.

(1) How does **absolute location** differ from **relative location**?

____

____

(2) What does the geographic theme of **place** describe about a location?

____

____

(3) The Midwest is one **region** of the United States. What characteristics make it a **region**?

____

____

(4) How can you see the theme of **movement** in a city like Washington, D.C.?

____

____

(5) How does **human-environment interaction** affect your life?

____

____

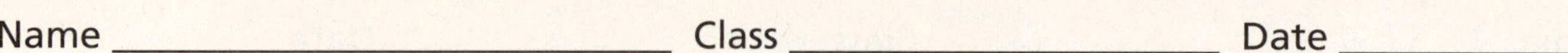

Name _____________________________ Class _____________________________ Date ____________

Core Concepts 1.3: Word Wise

Vocabulary Quiz Show Some quiz shows ask a question and expect the contestant to give the answer. In other shows, the contestant is given an answer and must supply the question. If the blank is in the question column, write the question that would result in the answer given. If the question is supplied, write the appropriate answer.

QUESTION	ANSWER
1 What do you call photographs taken from airplanes or helicopters?	**1** ____________________________
2 ____________________________	**2** scale
3 What is the name for a computer-based system that stores and uses information linked to geographic locations?	**3** ____________________________
4 ____________________________	**4** satellite images
5 What do you call a flat map of Earth's round surface?	**5** ____________________________
6 ____________________________	**6** distortion

Core Concepts 1.4: Word Wise

Crossword Puzzle The clues describe key terms from this section. Fill in the numbered *Across* boxes with the correct key terms. Then, do the same with the *Down* clues.

Across	Down
1. a map that shows an enlarged view of one part of the main map	4. a standard map diagram that shows the cardinal directions
2. the map part that shows how much space on the map represents a given distance	
3. the map part that shows what the map symbols mean	

Name _______________________________ Class _______________________________ Date ____________

Core Concepts 1.5: Word Wise

Sentence Builder Complete the sentences using the information you learned in this section. Be sure to include terminal punctuation.

① **Elevation** refers to the _______________________________

____

____

② A **special-purpose map** may show such things as _______________

____

____

③ A **political map** of your state would show _______________

____

____

④ A **physical map** shows _______________

____

____

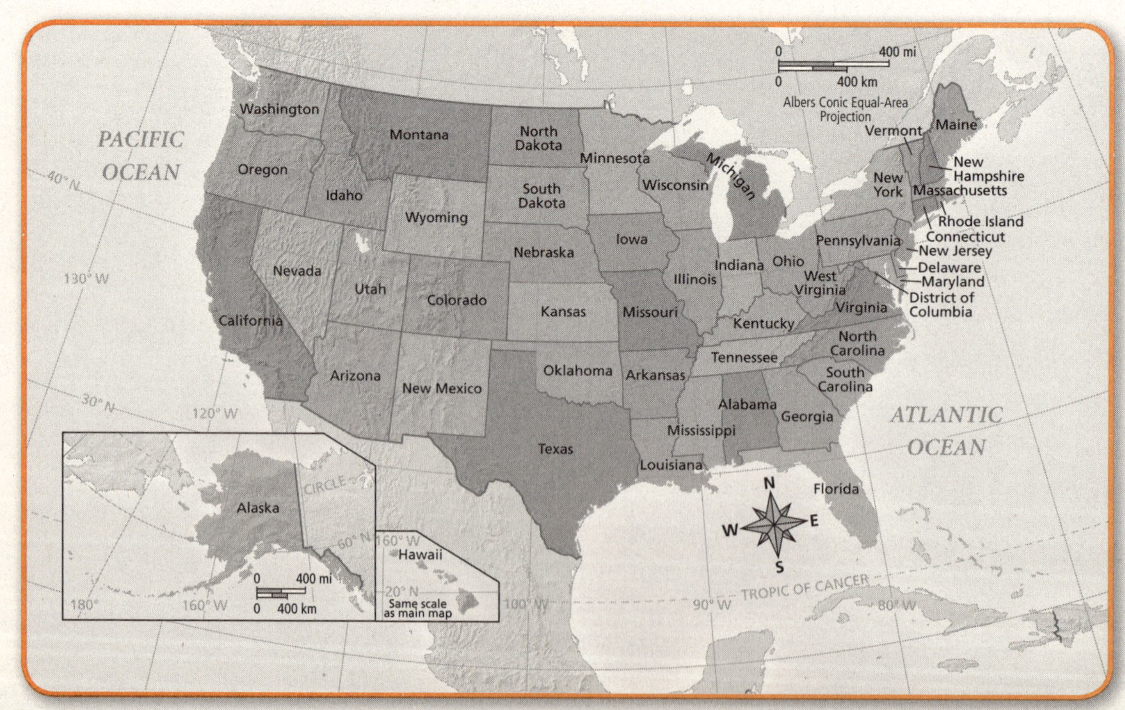

Sum It Up

Map Your Classroom Apply what you have learned about the tools of geography to your life by drawing a map of your classroom. Include a key and a compass rose. Use a tape measure or yardstick to make a scale bar. Draw a locator map to show the location of your classroom within your school.

Use the theme of place to describe the relative location of your classroom.

____

____

____

Name _________________________________ Class _________________________________ Date ____________

Core Concepts 2.1: Word Wise

Sentence Builder Complete the sentences using the information you learned in this section. Include terminal punctuation.

① Earth moves around the sun in an **orbit** that takes ____________________

days to ____

② The months of ____________________ and ____________________ have

the ____________________ and ____________________ **equinoxes,**

which are ____

③ It takes Earth ____________________ to complete a **revolution,** which is

____

④ The ____________________ and ____________________ **solstices,** which

occur during the months of ____________________ and

____________________, are _______________________________________

⑤ Earth ____________________ on its **axis,** which is an imaginary

____

Name _________________________________ Class _____________________________ Date _____________

Core Concepts 2.2: Word Wise

Words In Context For each question below, write an answer that shows your understanding of the boldfaced key term.

(1) How does Earth's **rotation** differ from its revolution?

____

____

____

(2) Why does Earth have multiple **time zones**?

____

____

____

Name _________________________ Class _________________________ Date ____________

Core Concepts 2.3: Word Wise

Vocabulary Quiz Show Some quiz shows ask a question and expect the contestant to give the answer. In other shows, the contestant is given an answer and must supply the question. If the blank is in the question column, write the question that would result in the answer given. If the question is supplied, write the appropriate answer.

QUESTION

ANSWER

1. _________________________

1. core

2. What do you call the thick layer of gases that surround our planet and make life possible?

2. _________________________

3. _________________________

3. mantle

4. What gets created by the physical processes that change Earth's surface by pushing its crust up or wearing it down?

4. _________________________

5. _________________________

5. crust

Name _________________________ Class _________________________ Date _________

Core Concepts 2.4: Word Wise

Crossword Puzzle The clues describe key terms from this section. Fill in the numbered *Across* boxes with the correct key terms. Then, do the same with the *Down* clues.

Across

1. when water, ice, or wind remove small pieces of rock
2. a stretch of low land between mountains, often formed by a river
3. occurs when running water picks up material from one place and leaves it in another
4. a high area with a flat top and at least one steep side

Down

5. flat plains formed on the seabed where a river deposits material over many years
6. a large area of flat or gently rolling land
7. wearing down rocks by chemical or mechanical means

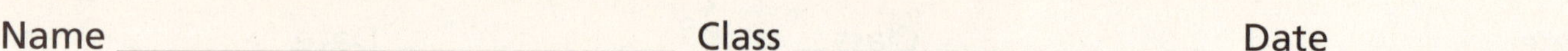

Core Concepts 2.5: Word Wise

Word Bank Choose one word from the word bank to fill in each blank. When you have finished, you will have a short summary of important ideas from the section.

Word Bank

magma	plates
faults	plate tectonics

Earth's crust is broken up into many huge blocks called

_________________________. According to the theory of _________________________,

these blocks slide and grind against one another. The places where their

edges meet are called _________________________, and this is where volcanoes

often form. When a volcano erupts, _________________________, which is melted

rock from deep within Earth, pours out onto the crust. Once it comes out of

the volcano, it is called lava.

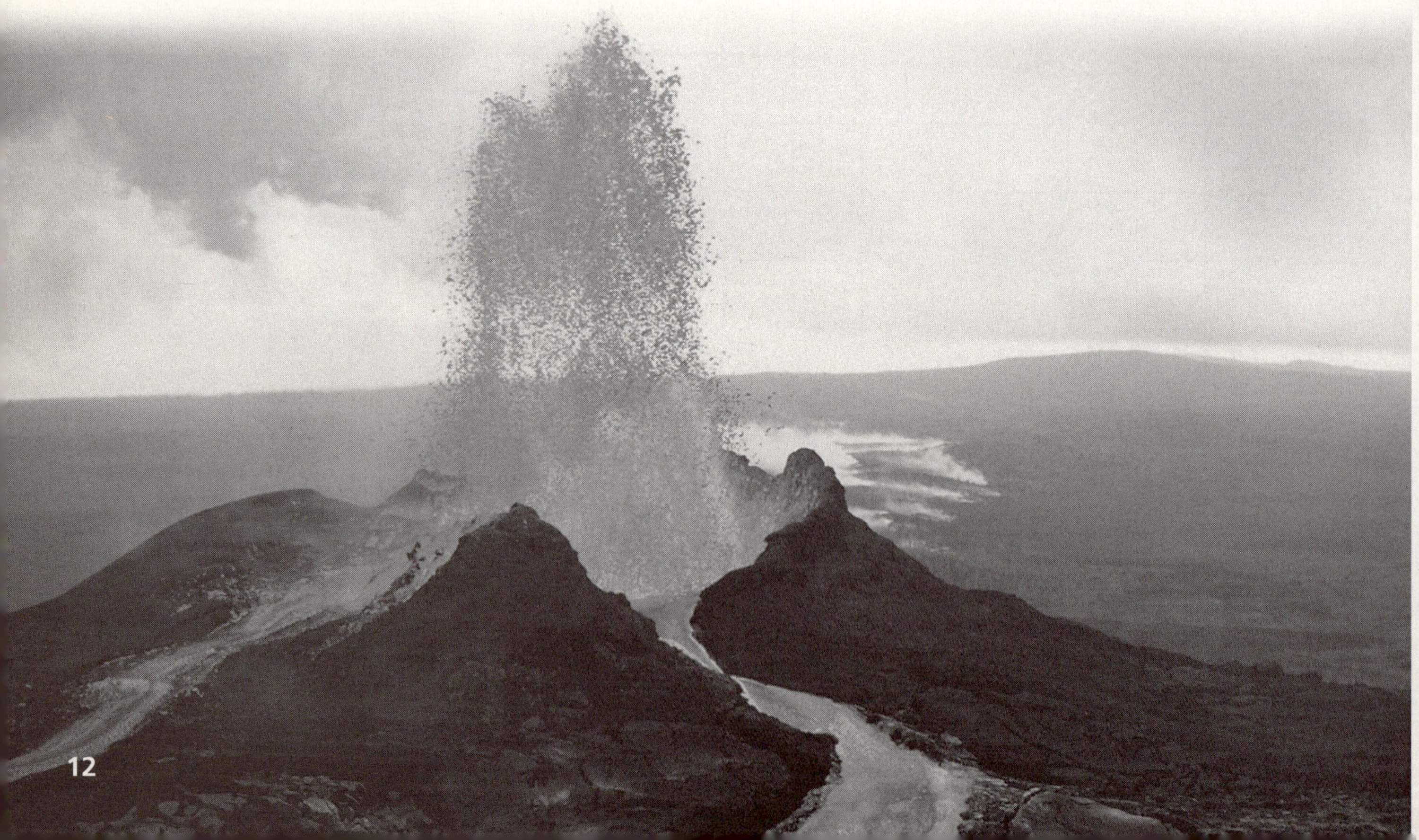

Name _________________________ Class _________________________ Date __________

Sum It Up

Label the Diagram Mark these physical features in the appropriate areas on the diagram below.

river valley   plateau
delta   mountains

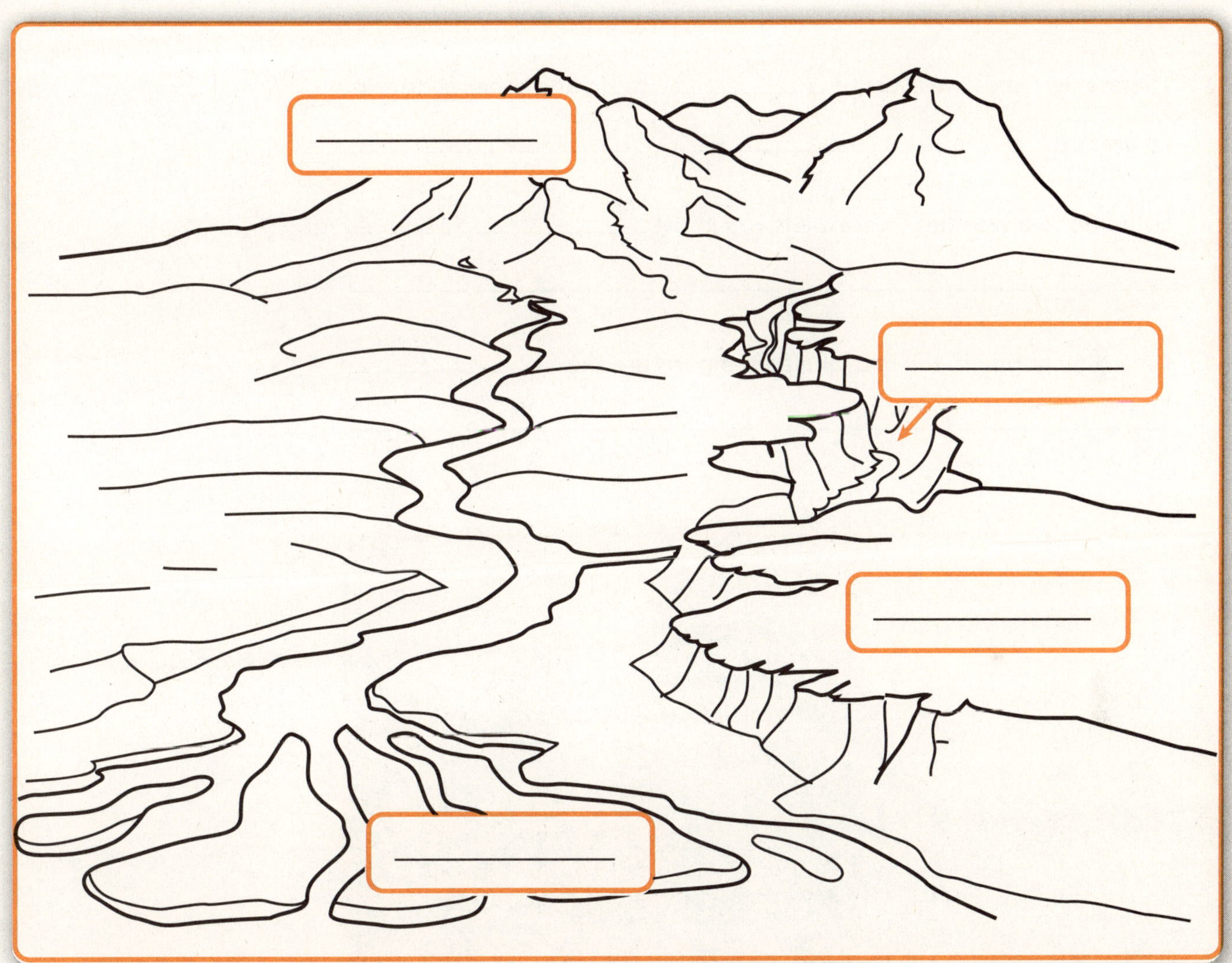

Name three forces that create these features. Explain how each one works.

____

____

____

Name ________________________________ Class ____________________________ Date ____________

Core Concepts 3.1: Word Wise

Sentence Builder Complete the sentences using the information you learned in this section. Include terminal punctuation.

(1) Types of **precipitation** include ______________________________________

____

(2) **Climate** describes the average ________________ and other factors in

an area ____

(3) Listening to a **weather** forecast lets you know ____________________

____

(4) On a climate graph, the line labeled **temperature** shows ____________

____

Name ______________________________   Class ______________________________   Date __________

Core Concepts 3.2: Word Wise

Crossword Puzzle The clues describe key terms from this section. Fill in the numbered *Across* boxes with the correct key terms. Then, do the same with the *Down* clues.

Across

1. name for the areas that lie north of the Arctic Circle and south of the Antarctic Circle
2. term describing the area between high and low latitudes
3. another name for the high latitudes
4. where the sun stays overhead or nearly overhead all year long

Down

5. height above sea level
6. another name for the middle latitudes
7. term for the area between the Tropic of Cancer and the Tropic of Capricorn

Core Concepts 3.3: Word Wise

Word Bank Choose one word from the word bank to fill in each blank. When you have finished, you will have a short summary of important ideas from the section.

Word Bank

evaporation   water cycle

Water, in one form or another, is constantly moving from Earth's

surface into the atmosphere and back to the surface. This process is called

the ___________________ and consists of four stages. The first stage is

___________________, when water from a puddle, river, or sea changes

into water vapor. Then it rises into the sky. The vapor condenses into clouds

high in the atmosphere. The vapor eventually cools, forms droplets or

snowflakes, and falls to the ground as rain or snow. The precipitation is then

absorbed by the ground or a body of water, where it will start the water

cycle all over again.

Name _______________________________   Class _______________________   Date ___________

Core Concepts 3.4: Word Wise

Words In Context For each question below, write an answer that shows your understanding of the boldfaced key term.

(1) How might people prepare for a **tropical cyclone**?

____

____

____

(2) Why do people fear **tornadoes**?

____

____

____

(3) What is one reason that precipitation is so heavy in the **intertropical convergence zone**?

____

____

____

(4) What weather conditions would you expect to see if a **hurricane** struck your region?

____

____

____

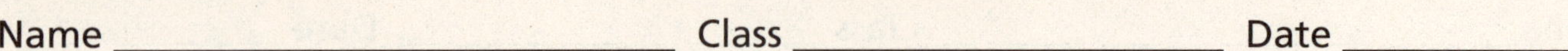

Core Concepts 3.5: Word Wise

Word Bank Choose one word from the word bank to fill in each blank.
When you have finished, you will have a short summary of important ideas
from the section.

Word Bank

tropical wet	tropical wet and dry
semiarid	arid
maritime	humid subtropical
subarctic	tundra

Earth has many climate types. Each one has a unique set of temperature

ranges, kinds of precipitation, and prevailing winds. Areas near the Equator

have a _______________ climate, which is a type of climate much

wetter than the _______________ climate. The desert

_______________ climate is found in places where there it is generally

hot with little precipitation. The _______________ climate has wet

summers and dry winters affected by the movement of the sun and shifting

bands of rain over the Equator.

In cold, dry areas in far northern North America and Asia, the

_______________ climate is characterized by cool summers and bitterly

cold, dry winters. _______________ climates also have cool summers

and very cold winters but have more precipitation, which allows pine trees

to grow.

In areas where moist winds bring precipitation from the ocean, the

climate is described as _______________. In these areas, winters are

mild and summers are hot. This is different from the _______________

climate, which also exists where winds are moist. However, this type of

climate has cool summers.

Name _______________________________   Class _______________________________   Date _____________

Core Concepts 3.6: Word Wise

Vocabulary Quiz Show Some quiz shows ask a question and expect the contestant to give the answer. In other shows, the contestant is given an answer and must supply the question. If the blank is in the question column, write the question that would result in the answer given. If the question is supplied, write the appropriate answer.

QUESTION

1. What do you call a grassland found in a tropical area with dry spells?

2. _______________________________

3. What is an interdependent community formed by plants and animals sharing an environment?

4. _______________________________

ANSWER

1. _______________________________

2. deciduous trees

3. _______________________________

4. coniferous trees

Sum It Up

Make Connections Use the text and maps from this section to fill in the circles of this concept web. Describe the features of a tropical wet and dry climate.

1. Temperature

2. Latitudes and hemispheres

3. Precipitation

4. Air patterns

5. Connected ecosystems

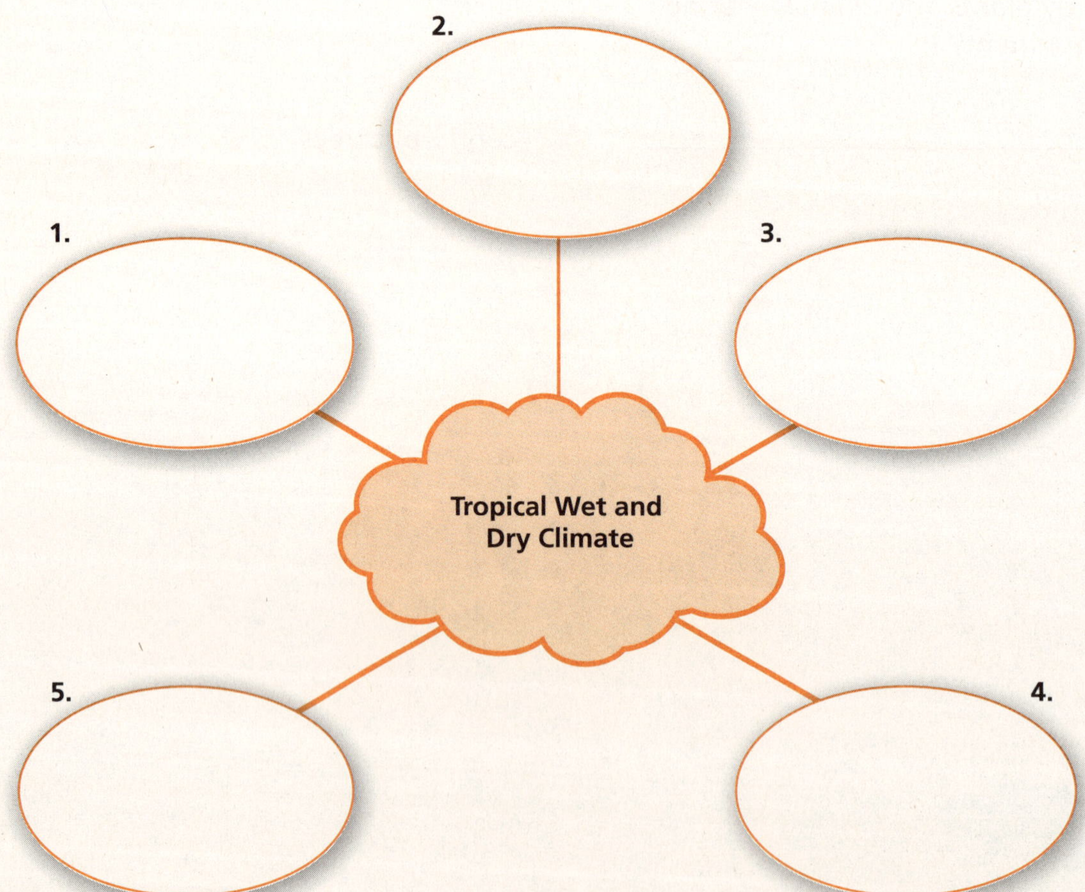

Name _______________________________   Class _____________________________   Date ____________

Core Concepts 4.1: Word Wise

Words In Context For each question below, write an answer that shows your understanding of the boldfaced key term.

(1) Why are trees considered a **renewable resource**?

____

____

(2) What makes water an important **natural resource**?

____

____

(3) Where do **fossil fuels** get their name?

____

____

(4) Name three factors that the **nonrenewable resources** of coal and petroleum have in common.

____

____

Name _______________________________ Class _______________________________ Date ____________

Core Concepts 4.2: Word Wise

Word Map Follow the model below to make a word map. The key term *colonization* is in the center oval. Write the definition in your own words at the upper left. In the upper right, list Characteristics, which means words or phrases that relate to the term. At the lower left list Noncharacteristics, which means words and phrases that would not be associated with it. In the lower right, draw a picture of the key term or use it in a sentence.

Definition in your own words	Characteristics
When settlers move to a region, they change it by bringing with them living things (like horses) and ideas (like music and religion).	• people starting farms • people putting up buildings and roads • people introducing plants and animals in a new area

colonization

NonCharacteristics	Picture or Sentence
• wilderness • any place untouched by humans • plants and animals that are native to the area	When people move into an area, they bring their plants, animals, ideas, and culture with them. This changes the area forever.

Now use the word map below to explore the meaning of the word *industrialization.* You may use your student text, a dictionary, and/or a thesaurus to complete each of the four sections.

Definition in your own words	Characteristics

industrialization

NonCharacteristics	Picture or Sentence

Make a word map of your own on a separate piece of paper for the word *suburbs.*

Name _________________________ Class ___________________________ Date ____________

Core Concepts 4.3: Word Wise

Sentence Builder Complete the sentences using the information you learned in this section. Be sure to include terminal punctuation.

(1) **Deforestation** is the result of ________________________________

____

(2) Air **pollution** occurs when ________________________________

____

(3) In an area with **biodiversity,** you would expect ________________

____

(4) A child with asthma who lives in an area with smog may suffer from

spillover because ____

____

Sum It Up

Make Connections Use what you learned in this section to answer these questions.

1. Think about how land use has changed since the 1800s. How do you think the world's supply of nonrenewable resources has been affected by these changes?

   ____

   ____

   ____

2. Imagine that a forest is being cut down to make room for new homes, farms, and roads. If a change in biodiversity takes place, is that an example of a spillover? Explain.

   ____

   ____

   ____

3. How is using public transportation like buses and subways a way to conserve energy?

   ____

   ____

   ____

4. Do you think building new suburbs helps or hurts the environment? Support your answer with evidence from the text or your personal experience.

   ____

   ____

   ____

Name ______________________________   Class ____________________   Date __________

Core Concepts 5.1: Word Wise

Vocabulary Quiz Show Some quiz shows ask a question and expect the contestant to give the answer. In other shows, the contestant is given an answer and must supply the question. If the blank is in the question column, write the question that would result in the answer given. If the question is supplied, write the appropriate answer.

QUESTION	ANSWER
(1) _______________________________	(1) incentive
(2) What describes the value of what you decide to give up when you make an economic choice?	(2) _______________________________
(3) _______________________________	(3) economics
(4) What do you call the amount of goods or services available for use?	(4) _______________________________
(5) _______________________________	(5) consumers
(6) What word describes the degree of desire for a good or a service?	(6) _______________________________
(7) _______________________________	(7) producers
(8) What is the term for having a limited quantity of resources to meet unlimited wants?	(8) _______________________________

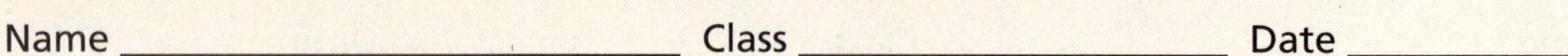

Core Concepts 5.2: Word Wise

Crossword Puzzle The clues describe key terms from this section. Fill in the numbered *Across* boxes with the correct key terms. Then, do the same with the *Down* clues.

Across	Down
1. an organized way for goods and services to be exchanged	5. a decline in economic growth for six or more months in a row
2. the money earned by selling goods and services	6. a general increase in prices over time
3. the act of a company concentrating on just a few goods or services	
4. the money left after subtracting the costs of doing business	

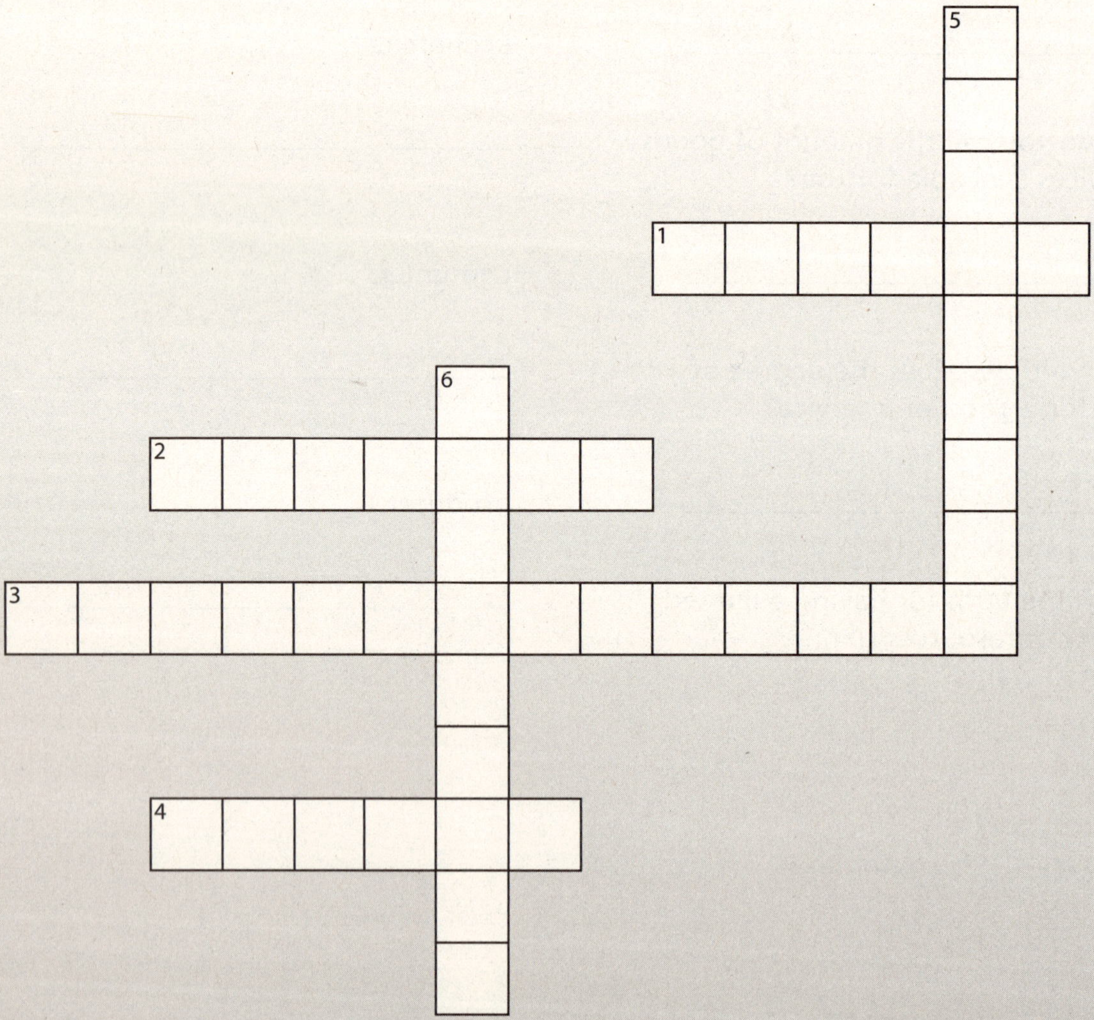

Name ___________________________ Class ___________________________ Date ___________

Core Concepts 5.3: Word Wise

Words In Context For each question below, write an answer that shows your understanding of the boldfaced key term.

1. What makes a person's way of life important in a **traditional economy**?

____

____

____

2. Who makes economic decisions in a **mixed economy** and why?

____

____

____

3. How do new businesses benefit from the freedom of a **market economy**?

____

____

____

4. How does a **command economy** differ from a market economy?

____

____

____

Name ___________________________ Class ___________________________ Date ___________

Core Concepts 5.4: Word Wise

Word Map Follow the model below to make a word map. The key term *developed country* is in the center oval. Write the definition in your own words at the upper left. In the upper right, list Characteristics, which means words or phrases that relate to the term. At the lower left list Noncharacteristics, which means words and phrases that would not be associated with it. In the lower right, draw a picture of the key term or use it in a sentence.

Definition in your own words	**Characteristics**
a nation with a strong economy and a high standard of living such as Japan	• United States, Japan, Australia, many European nations • people have access to a lot of goods and services • people have medical care, homes, and wages

developed country

Noncharacteristics	**Picture or Sentence**
• developing country—a nation with a less productive economy and low standard of living such as Haiti • people struggle to have the basic necessities of life (food, clean water, shelter, and medical care)	Developed countries' strong economies are responsible for the high standard of living their people. Developing countries want to create strong economies for this reason.

Now use the word map below to explore the meaning of the word *technology*. You may use your student text, a dictionary, and/or a thesaurus to complete each of the four sections.

Definition in your own words	**Characteristics**

technology

Noncharacteristics	**Picture or Sentence**

Make word maps of your own on a separate piece of paper for these words: *development, gross domestic product,* and *productivity.*

Name _______________________________ Class _____________________ Date ____________

Core Concepts 5.5: Word Wise

Sentence Builder Complete the sentences using the information you learned in this section. Include terminal punctuation.

(1) Grain is one example of an **export** from the United States because it is

____

(2) You might **trade** your _____________________ for _____________________

____

(3) Consumers benefit from **free trade** because _____________________

____

(4) China **imports** _____________________ from _____________________

____

(5) An example of a **tariff** is a _____________________

____

(6) The purpose of a **trade barrier** is _____________________

____

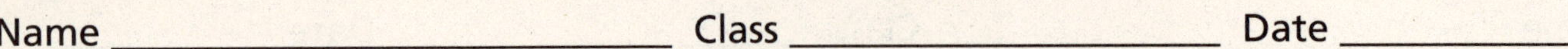

Core Concepts 5.6: Word Wise

Word Bank Choose one word from the word bank to fill in each blank.
When you have finished, you will have a short summary of important ideas
from the section.

Word Bank

budget	credit
interest	invest
stocks	bonds
saving	

You have options for using your money wisely. For example,

_________________ funds in a bank, credit union, or other financial

institution ensures that you will have money for future use. You can take

some of that money and _________________ it. Hopefully this will earn

you a profit. One way to do this is to buy _________________, which are

certificates from a business or the government promising to pay back your

money plus additional money. Another way to do it is to purchase

_________________, which give you shares of ownership in a company.

Of course, people also buy expensive things such as a car or a home

even though they do not have enough money to pay for it in full. To do this,

most people use _________________. This means that they agree to pay

for their purchase over time. As they pay back the loan, they will also have

to pay _________________. If this seems complex, don't worry. You can

create and stick to a money-management plan called a(n)

_________________. It will help you to save more and to avoid borrowing

too much money.

Name _______________________________   Class ___________________________   Date ____________

Sum It Up

Think About It Use what you learned in this section to answer these questions about Myra and the way she uses her money.

(1) Your friend Myra is given $100. She wants to invest half of it so she can earn some more money. What do you think is the best way for her to do this? Why?

____

____

____

(2) Myra plans to use the other $50 to buy a new pair of headphones. How might competition and specialization among headphone producers affect her choice?

____

____

____

(3) Assume that Myra lives in a command economy. How do you think her headphone choices might be different from those in a market economy?

____

____

____

(4) Now assume that Myra lives in a developing country. How might the supply and demand for $50 headphones be different than in a developed country?

____

____

____

Core Concepts 6.1: Word Wise

Word Bank Choose one word from the word bank to fill in each blank. When you have finished, you will have a short summary of important ideas from the section.

Word Bank

demographers   birth rate

infant mortality rate   death rate

There are many ways to investigate and measure an area's population growth. For example, a country's ____________________, or the number of live births per 1,000 people in a year, is an important measurement.

____________________, the scientists who study human populations, often compare this number to the ____________________, which is the number of deaths per 1,000 people in a year.

When the birth rate is higher than the death rate, the population is growing. But when the death rate is higher than the birth rate, the population does not grow. Such slowdowns in population often take place when people do not have enough food and clean water. A lack of food and clean water often leads to a higher ____________________, which is the number of infant deaths per 1,000 births.

Name _______________________________ Class _____________________________ Date ____________

Core Concepts 6.2: Word Wise

Words In Context For each question below, write an answer that shows your understanding of the boldfaced key term.

(1) Think of what a typical U.S. town or city is like on a busy Saturday afternoon, when many people are running errands, shopping, and participating in other activities. Which parts of a town do you think have the highest and lowest **population density** on a typical Saturday?

____

____

____

____

(2) How do you think changes in transportation over the past 100 years have changed **population distribution**?

____

____

____

____

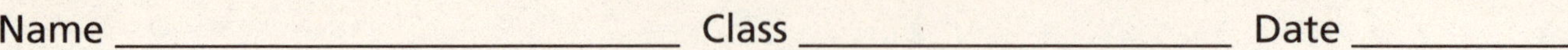

Core Concepts 6.3: Word Wise

Word Map Follow the model below to make a word map. The key term *migration* is in the center oval. Write the definition in your own words at the upper left. In the upper right, list Characteristics, which means words or phrases that relate to the term. At the lower left list Noncharacteristics, which means words and phrases that would not be associated with it. In the lower right, draw a picture of the key term or use it in a sentence.

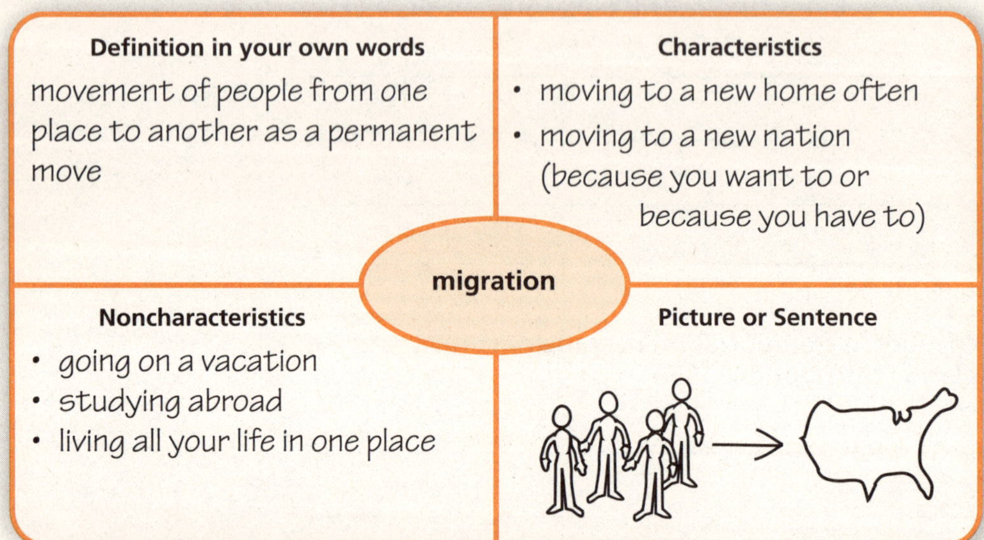

Now use the word map below to explore the meaning of the key term *push factor*. You may use your student text, a dictionary, and/or a thesaurus to complete each of the four sections.

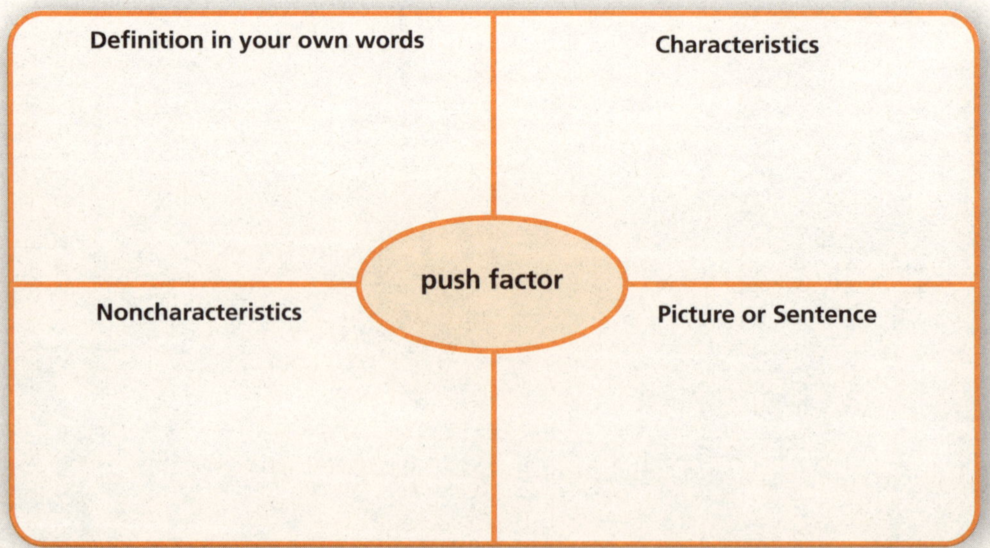

Make word maps of your own on a separate piece of paper for the following words: *emigrate*, *immigrate*, and *pull factor*.

Name _________________________ Class _____________________ Date ____________

Core Concepts 6.4: Word Wise

Vocabulary Quiz Show Some quiz shows ask a question and expect the contestant to give the answer. In other shows, the contestant is given an answer and must supply the question. If the blank is in the question column, write the question that would result in the answer given. If the question is supplied, write the appropriate answer.

QUESTION	ANSWER
(1) What do you call a poor, overcrowded urban area?	(1) _________________________
(2) _________________________	(2) urbanization
(3) What occurs when the population of a city begins to spread away from the center of the city?	(3) _________________________
(4) _________________________	(4) rural
(5) A city is what type of area?	(5) _________________________

Sum It Up

Predict Imagine that you are a demographer. The mayor of a city that has recently experienced rapid population growth has asked you to investigate why his region is growing so quickly. Use what you learned in this section to predict three reasons for any city's growth.

1. _______________________
   ____
2. _______________________
   ____
3. _______________________
   ____

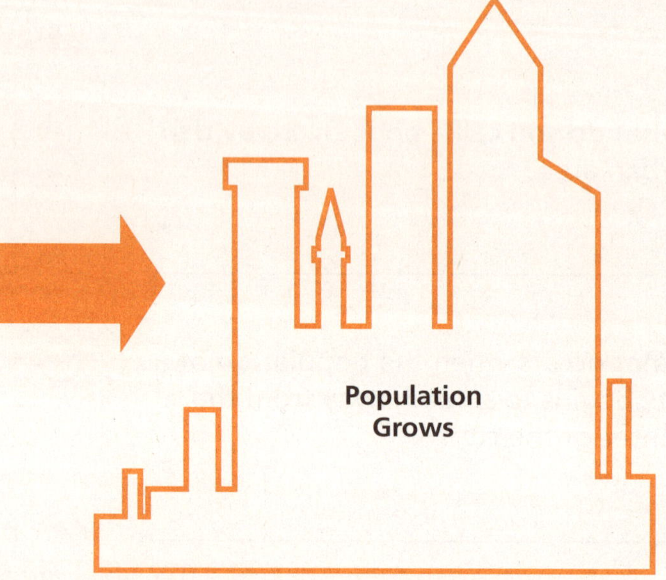

Now imagine that the mayor of a city that has recently seen its population decrease has asked for your help. Use what you learned in this section to predict three reasons for any city's drop in population.

1. _______________________
   ____
2. _______________________
   ____
3. _______________________
   ____

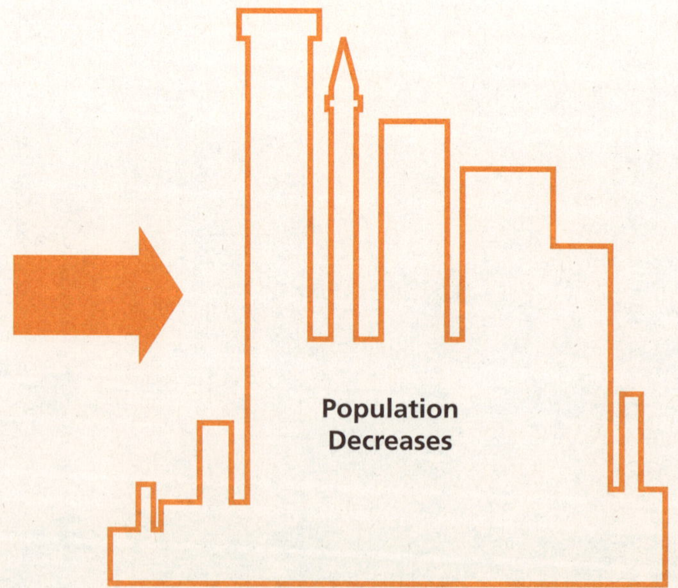

Name ___________________________ Class ___________________________ Date ___________

Core Concepts 7.1: Word Wise

Sentence Builder Complete the sentences using the information you learned in this section. Include terminal punctuation.

(1) In modern American culture, one example of a **norm** is _______________

____

(2) Examples of **cultural traits** are language, _______________________

____

(3) Human activities define the **cultural landscape** by _______________

____

(4) A nation's **culture** includes its _______________________________

____

(5) A **culture region** can extend beyond a nation's borders because ______

____

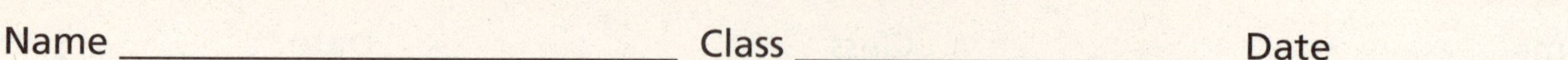

Core Concepts 7.2: Word Wise

Vocabulary Quiz Show Some quiz shows ask a question and expect the contestant to give the answer. In other shows, the contestant is given an answer and must supply the question. If the blank is in the question column, write the question that would result in the answer given. If the question is supplied, write the appropriate answer.

QUESTION	ANSWER
(1) What is the basic unit of any society?	(1) _____________________
(2) _____________________	(2) nuclear family
(3) What word describes a human group that meets its basic needs in a shared culture?	(3) _____________________
(4) _____________________	(4) extended family
(5) What term describes people who share the same standard of living based on their economic status?	(5) _____________________
(6) _____________________	(6) social structure

Name ___________________________   Class _____________________   Date ___________

Core Concepts 7.3: Word Wise

Word Map Follow the model below to make a word map. The key term *communicate* is in the center oval. Write the definition in your own words at the upper left. In the upper right, list characteristics, which means words or phrases that relate to the term. At the lower left list noncharacteristics, which means words and phrases that would not be associated with it. In the lower right, draw a picture of the key term or use it in a sentence.

Definition in your own words

When you communicate, you pass along information that someone else can understand.

Characteristics

- convey information
- spread news
- understand others

communicate

Noncharacteristics

- withhold information
- conceal facts
- not understand what others are saying
- not knowing the language of an area
- saying things that confuse others

Picture or Sentence

Now use the word map below to explore the meaning of the word *language*. You may use your student text, a dictionary, and/or a thesaurus to complete each of the four sections.

Definition in your own words

Characteristics

language

Noncharacteristics

Picture or Sentence

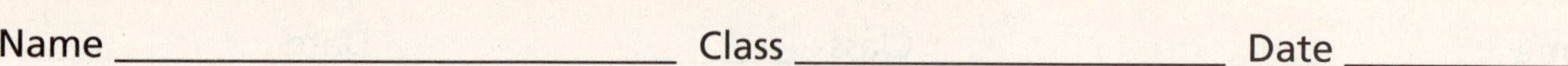

Core Concepts 7.4: Word Wise

Words In Context For each question below, write an answer that shows your understanding of the boldfaced key term.

① Why do many people value **religion**, and what do they hope to gain from it?

____

____

____

② Which situation would test your **ethics**: learning how to drive a car or deciding whether or not to copy someone else's homework? Explain.

____

____

____

Name _______________________ Class _______________________ Date ___________

Core Concepts 7.5: Word Wise

Crossword Puzzle The clues describe key terms from this section. Fill in the numbered *Across* boxes with the correct key terms. Then, do the same with the *Down* clues.

Across	Down
1. an art form that uses sound	4. written works of art
2. an idea reflected in artwork that relates to the whole world	5. a person who designs buildings
3. the process of designing and constructing buildings	6. works of art that are seen instead of read or heard

Core Concepts 7.6: Word Wise

Sentence Builder Complete the sentences using the information you learned in this section. Include terminal punctuation.

1 Ideas such as _____________________ and _____________________ spread

outward from a **cultural hearth** when _________________________________

____

2 One example of **diversity** is ____

____

3 Traders were partially responsible for **cultural diffusion** because _______

____

Name _______________________________   Class _____________________________   Date ______________

Core Concepts 7.7: Word Wise

Word Bank Choose one word from the word bank to fill in each blank. When you have finished, you will have a short summary of important ideas from the section.

Word Bank

irrigate   science
technologies   standard of living

Throughout history, cultural development follows people's discoveries

about the natural world. New understandings in ___________________

helped ancient groups change from a life of hunting and gathering to

farming. For example, new ___________________ such as metalworking let

people create tools that helped them to clear land and to grow crops. When

people learned to ___________________ land, it increased the chances for

successful agriculture by making more land arable and providing some

protection against droughts.

As agriculture—and later industry—became central to world

economies, people were able to improve their ___________________ and

afford more goods and services.

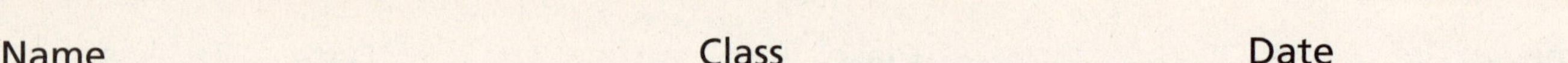

Name ________________________________ Class ____________________________ Date ___________

Sum It Up

Draw and Label Imagine that you have been given the chance to create a new town with new cultural elements. Draw a scene of everyday life in your new town, representing and labeling all of the concepts listed in the key.

KEY

A = cultural trait   **B** = language   **C** = art   **D** = technology

Answer these questions about your town on a separate piece of paper:

1. Describe the technology you included. How does it affect daily life in the town?

2. Describe diversity in the town. How does this diversity influence the town's overall culture?

44

Name _________________________ Class _________________________ Date ____________

Core Concepts 8.1: Word Wise

Sentence Builder Complete the sentences using the information you learned in this section. Include terminal punctuation.

(1) Two goals of a **government** are _______________________________

____

(2) A **constitution** is a system _______________________________

____

(3) In a **limited government,** _______________________________

____

(4) In an **unlimited government,** _______________________________

____

(5) **Tyranny** can result in an abuse of power such as _______________

____

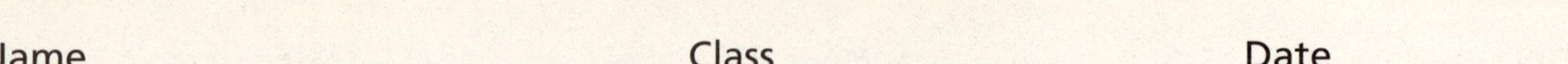

Core Concepts 8.2: Word Wise

Crossword Puzzle The clues describe key terms from this section. Fill in the numbered *Across* boxes with the correct key terms. Then, do the same with the *Down* clues.

Across	Down
1. In the political system called ________________, the government owns all the property.	5. another name for a nation or country
2. One person or a small group holds all the power in a(n) ________________ government.	6. A(n) ________________ consists of several nations or territories and may be quite large.
3. In a(n) ________________, the citizens have political power.	7. a country led by a king or a queen
4. A city and surrounding area that form an independent state is a(n) ________________.	

Name _____________________________ Class _____________________________ Date ____________

Core Concepts 8.3: Word Wise

Word Map Follow the model below to make a word map. The term *unitary system* is in the center oval. Write the definition in your own words at the upper left. In the upper right, list Characteristics, which means words or phrases that relate to the term. At the lower left list Noncharacteristics, which means words and phrases that would not be associated with it. In the lower right, draw a picture of the key term or use it in a sentence.

Definition in your own words

a central government that makes laws for the whole country

Characteristics

- single government
- centralized government
- most nations today

unitary system

Noncharacteristics

- federal system
- divided government
- confederal system
- United States

Picture or Sentence

A country with a unitary system has a very powerful central government.

Now use the word map below to explore the meaning of the term *federal system*. You may use your student text, a dictionary, and/or a thesaurus to complete each of the four sections.

Definition in your own words

Characteristics

federal system

Noncharacteristics

Picture or Sentence

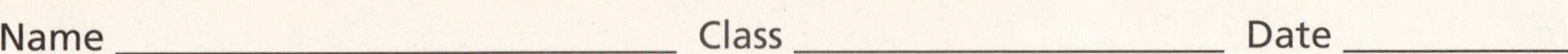

Core Concepts 8.4: Word Wise

Words In Context For each question below, write an answer that shows your understanding of the boldfaced key term.

1. How is a **treaty** an example of international cooperation?

   ____

   ____

   ____

2. How does **foreign policy** affect both the country that makes it and other countries?

   ____

   ____

   ____

3. How might a nation's foreign policy protect its **sovereignty**?

   ____

   ____

   ____

4. How are an American president's visits to foreign nations important for **diplomacy**?

   ____

   ____

   ____

Name _________________________ Class _________________ Date __________

Core Concepts 8.5: Word Wise

Word Bank Choose one word from the word bank to fill in each blank. When you have finished, you will have a short summary of important ideas from the section.

Word Bank

political party   civic life

citizens   civic participation

interest group

    People born in the United States or who have completed the

naturalization process are U.S. _________________. There are a number

of ways to take advantage of the privileges of citizenship. For example, you

may register to become a member of a _________________ that reflects

your political views. Becoming involved with this group and other

organizations is a simple, effective way of participating in

_________________. Voting, speaking out in meetings, signing petitions,

or simply staying informed are other kinds of _________________.

If there is a certain issue about which you feel strongly, you may want to

join a related _________________ dedicated to that particular cause.

Sum It Up

Predict Read each boldfaced statement. Think about what you read in this section. Then, consider the change given in the sentence starters. In each case you are making a logical prediction based on what you learned in this chapter. Include terminal punctuation.

1. **Country A is a representative democracy with a federal system of government.**

   If Country A switches to a unitary system of government, then ________

   ____

   ____

2. **Country B is made up of territory on one continent.**

   If Country B changes its foreign policy to become an overseas empire, then

   ____

   ____

3. **Country C has had the same constitution for 150 years.**

   If Country C's government becomes authoritarian, then ________

   ____

   ____

4. **Country D has a limited government made up of people from several political parties.**

   If Country D changes to unlimited government, then ________

   ____

   ____

5. **Country E has always encouraged the civic participation of its citizens.**

   If Country E's government becomes a tyranny, then ________

   ____

   ____

Name ______________________________   Class ______________________   Date ____________

Core Concepts 9.1: Word Wise

Crossword Puzzle The clues are definitions of key terms from this section.
Fill in the numbered *Across* boxes with the correct key terms. Then, do the
same with the *Down* clues.

Across	Down
1. a length of time that is important because of certain events or developments that occurred during that era	3. a person who studies, describes, and explains the past
2. a graphic organizer that shows events in the chronological order in which they happened	4. a list of events in the order in which they took place
	5. the time before humans invented writing

Name _______________________________ Class _____________________________ Date ____________

Core Concepts 9.2: Word Wise

Words In Context For each question below, write an answer that shows your understanding of the boldfaced key term.

1 Why is an article written about a famous explorer considered a **secondary source**?

____

____

____

2 Why do museums collect and display **artifacts**?

____

____

____

3 When researching a topic, why must you be on guard against **bias**?

____

____

____

4 If you were doing a project about a famous battle, what **primary sources** might you use?

____

____

____

Core Concepts 9.3: Word Wise

Word Bank Choose one word from the word bank to fill in each blank. When you have finished, you will have a short summary of important ideas from the section.

Word Bank

archaeology
anthropology
oral tradition

For centuries before people began to record information by writing,

history and culture was communicated to younger generations through

_____________________. By passing down information through songs and

storytelling, people were able to continue their traditions for hundreds

of years.

Today, people involved in the field of _____________________ study this

practice as well as other aspects of how different cultures developed. These

historians also depend on the findings of the people who work in

_____________________. Using evidence from artifacts, scientists in this field

determine how people behaved and what their culture was like.

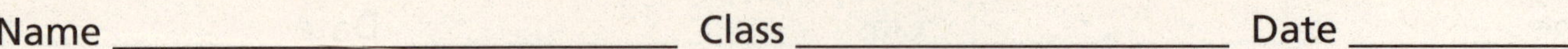

Core Concepts 9.4: Word Wise

Word Map Follow the model below to make a word map. The key term *locate* is in the center oval. Write the definition in your own words at the upper left. In the upper right, list Characteristics, which means words or phrases that relate to the term. At the lower left list Noncharacteristics, which means words and phrases that would not be associated with it. In the lower right, draw a picture of the key term or use it in a sentence.

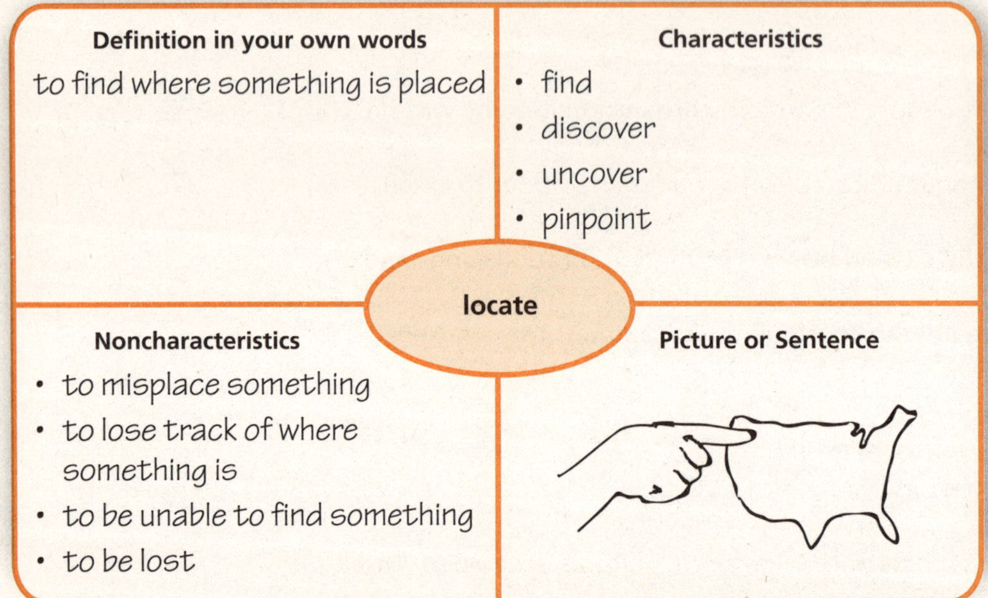

Definition in your own words

to find where something is placed

Characteristics

- find
- discover
- uncover
- pinpoint

locate

Noncharacteristics

- to misplace something
- to lose track of where something is
- to be unable to find something
- to be lost

Picture or Sentence

Now use the word map below to explore the meaning of the word *historical map*. You may use your student text, a dictionary, and/or a thesaurus to complete each of the four sections.

Definition in your own words

Characteristics

historical map

Noncharacteristics

Picture or Sentence

Name _______________________________ Class ____________________________ Date ____________

Sum It Up

Be a History Detective Imagine that it has just been revealed that a famous American was actually a spy for another country. You are a historian collecting information for a documentary about this American's secret life. Explain how you would use each type of resource listed in the table's column headings. Include a specific example of each kind of resource. (You will need to use your imagination for this part.)

Primary Sources	Secondary Sources	Artifacts

Essential Question

What are the challenges of diversity?

Preview Before you begin this chapter, think about the Essential Question. Understanding how the Essential Question connects to your life will help you understand the chapter you are about to read.

Connect to Your Life

(1) Think of a time when you learned about another culture. Name the other culture and tell at least one way in which it differed from yours.

____

____

(2) Think about some general ways that in which people express their differences in taste. Fill in the table below with your ideas.

Categories	Clothing	Food	Music	Interests
Expressions of Different Taste				

Connect to the Chapter

(3) Preview the chapter. Skim the headings, photos, and graphics. In the table below, predict the challenges that diversity presented to the people living in ancient and medieval Europe. One example is given in the table.

Type of Diversity	Ethnic	Religious	Political	Linguistic
Challenges			People with different values have different political viewpoints. The values and political ides may actually be exact opposites.	

(4) After reading the chapter, put a check mark next to your ideas that turned out to be correct.

Name _____________________________ Class _____________________________ Date ____________

Connect to myStory: Alexander the Great: A Prophecy Fulfilled

1 List the major events in your life up to now. You should write at least three.

____

____

____

2 List the major events of Alexander's life in the boxes of the chart.

The Life of Alexander the Great

Growing Up   **Fighting Persia**   **Building an Empire**

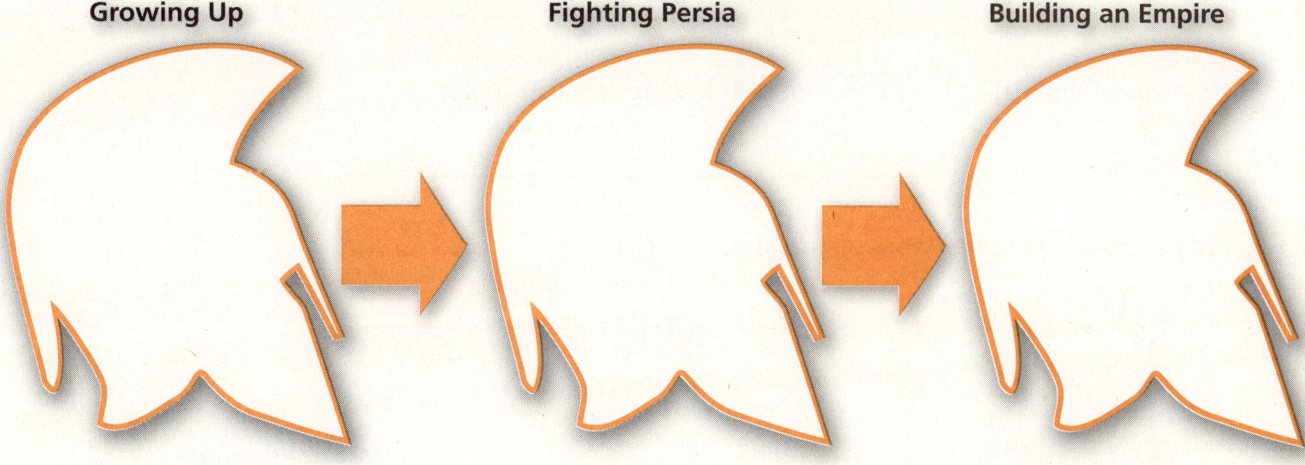

3 Look at the Growing Up box above. How do your life events differ from Alexander's early life events?

____

____

____

4 What might be the challenges of ruling an empire as big and diverse as the one Alexander the Great conquered?

____

____

____

Word Wise

Sentence Builder Complete the sentences using the information you learned in this section. Include terminal punctuation.

1. Greece is considered a **cultural hearth** because _____________________

____

2. Greek scholars started a branch of study called **philosophy** which

____

3. Two of the most famous Greek **city-states** were _____________________

____

4. In Athens, the male citizens took part in the world's first **direct**

democracy by ____

5. Some Greek city-states were **oligarchies**, which means ______________

____

Name _________________________ Class _________________________ Date __________

Take Notes

Map Skills Use the maps in *all* sections of this chapter to make a key and to label the Places to Know on the outline map below. Remember, in addition to this section, you will need to refer to Sections 2 through 4.

Places to Know!

Physical Features	Countries/Empires	City-States and Cities
Aegean Sea	Spain	Athens
Crete	Italy	Sparta
Peloponnesian Peninsula	Holy Roman Empire	Constantinople
Mediterranean Sea	France	Rome
Balkan Peninsula		Venice
Black Sea		

Essential Question

How did the diversity of Alexander the Great's Empire affect Greek culture?

____

____

____

Word Wise

Word Map Follow the model below to make a word map. The key term
patrician is in the center oval. Write the definition in your own words at the
upper left. In the upper right, list Characteristics, which means words or
phrases that relate to the term. At the lower left list Noncharacteristics,
which means words and phrases that would not be associated with it. In the
lower right, draw a picture of the key term or use it in a sentence.

Definition in your own words	Characteristics
rich man whose vote counted more than the common person's	• all the Senate consuls were patricians; they were the ones who passed the laws • owned land • male or female • important person
patrician	
Noncharacteristics	Picture or Sentence
• commoner; plebian • slave • someone poor who didn't own land • foreigner (non Roman)	The male patricians held the power in the Roman Republic because only they could be the consuls in the Senate.

Now use the word map below to explore the meaning of the word
representative democracy. You may use your student text, a dictionary,
and/or a thesaurus to complete each of the four sections.

Definition in your own words	Characteristics
representative democracy	
Noncharacteristics	Picture or Sentence

Make word maps of your own on a separate piece of paper for these key
terms: *Pax Romana* and *aqueduct.*

Name _________________________   Class ___________________   Date ___________

Take Notes

Sequence Record major events from the history of Ancient Rome on the
timeline below. Check the section to be sure you are putting the events in
chronological order.

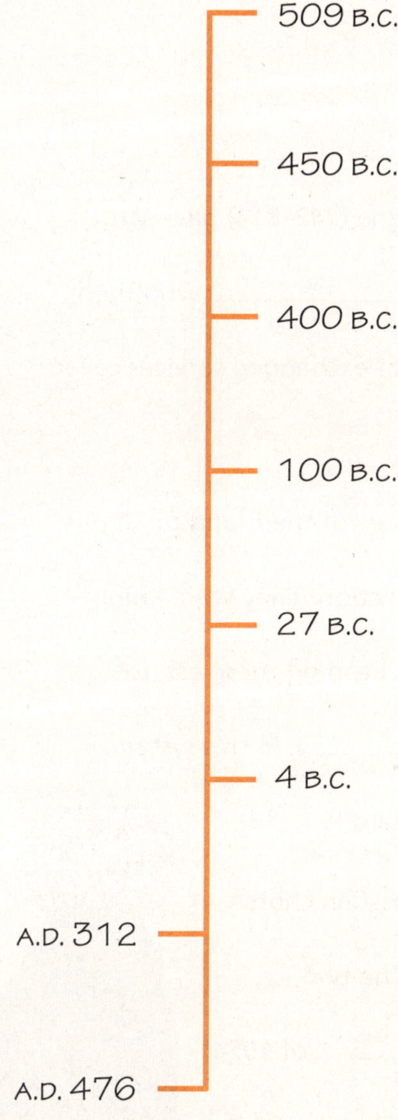

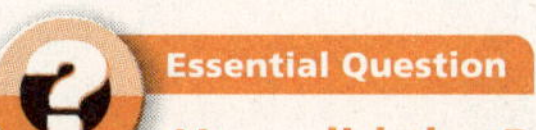
Essential Question

How did the Romans use citizenship to unify a diverse empire?

____

____

____

Word Wise

Word Bank Choose one word from the word bank to fill in each blank.
When you have finished, you will have a short summary of important ideas
from the section.

Word Bank

Schism   lords
vassals   feudalism
manorialism

In Western Europe, a ruler named Charlemagne (742–814) gave large

pieces of land as estates to nobles called __________________, who then

owed him services. This was the start of a system of exchanged services called

__________________.

The nobles who received estates then gave part of their land to

__________________ in exchange for their protection. They were knights

that gave military support to the nobles. Peasants lived on these estates

under the economic system called __________________. In this system,

peasants worked the land for the nobles who owned it.

Meanwhile, in the Byzantine empire, the Christian church

developed differently from the Church in Rome. The two

churches split apart in the Great __________________ of 1054.

After the division, there was the Roman Catholic Church and the

Greek Orthodox Church.

Name _________________________ Class _____________________ Date ___________

Take Notes

Summarize Use the information in your textbook to complete this graphic organizer. In the top three boxes, record details about the roles that the king, the lords, and the vassals played in feudalism. Then in the bottom box, write a few sentences summarizing how the system of feudalism worked.

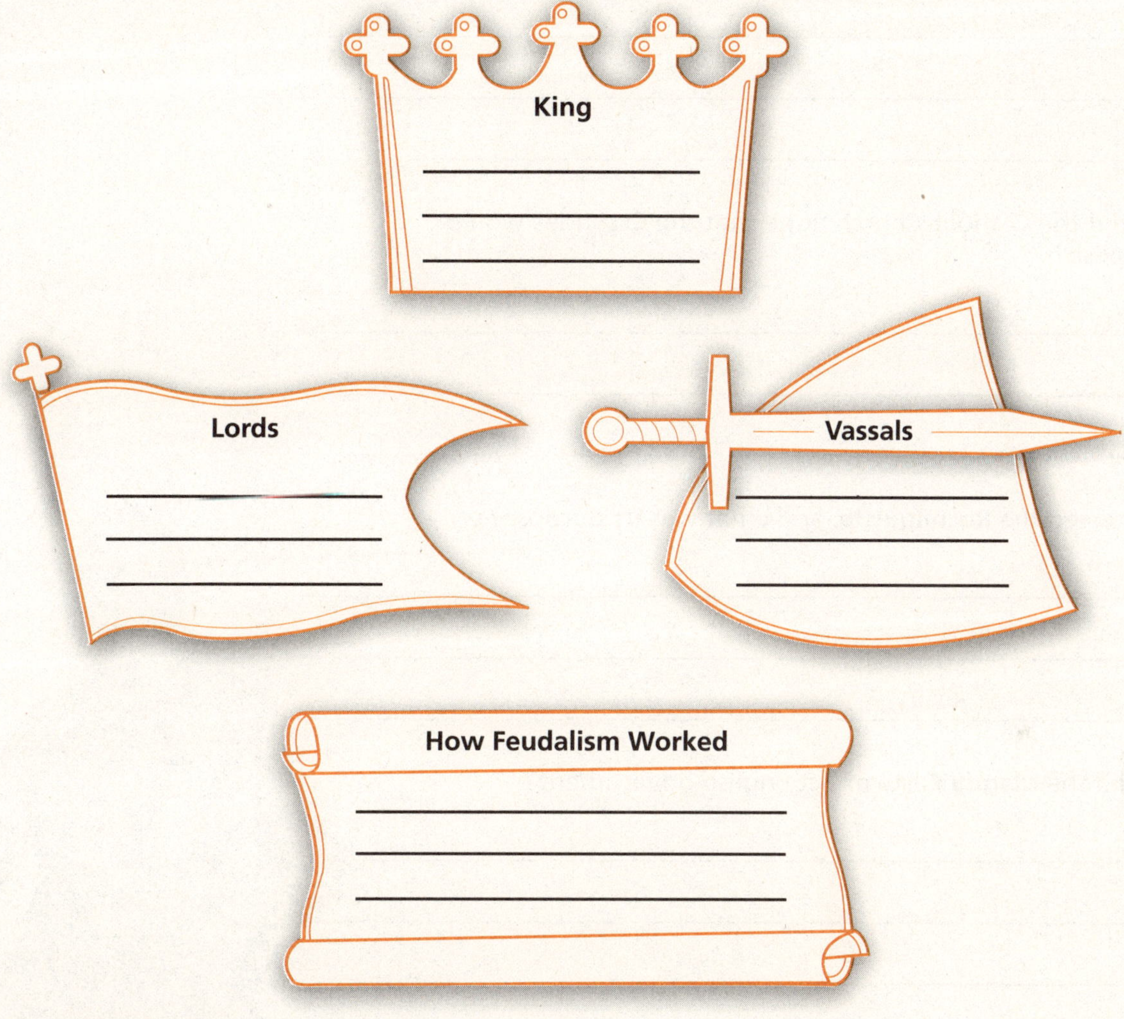

Essential Question

How did cultural differences between the East and the West affect the Christian church?

____

____

____

Name _______________________________ Class _______________________________ Date ___________

Word Wise

Words In Context For each question below, write an answer that shows your understanding of the boldfaced key term.

1. Why did the craftspeople form **guilds**?

   ____

   ____

   ____

2. What did the Catholic Church hope that the **Crusades** would accomplish?

   ____

   ____

   ____

3. Who started the **Reconquista**, and what was its purpose?

   ____

   ____

   ____

4. How did the **Magna Carta** affect English government?

   ____

   ____

   ____

Name _________________________ Class _________________________ Date _____________

Take Notes

Cause and Effect Use this cause-and-effect graphic organizer to record information about the Crusades and the decline of feudalism.

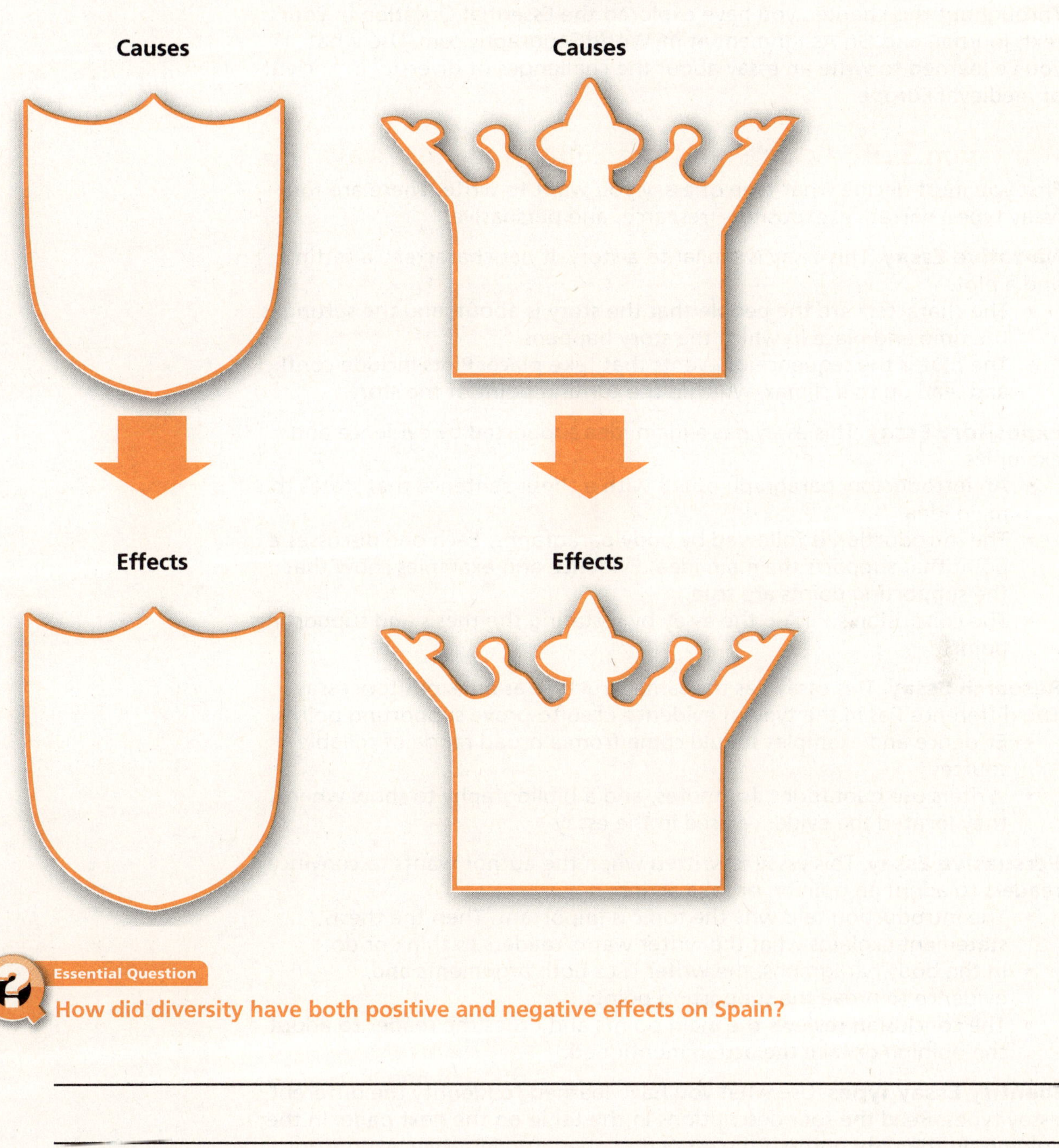

Essential Question

How did diversity have both positive and negative effects on Spain?

____

____

____

What are the challenges of diversity?

Prepare to Write

Throughout this chapter, you have explored the Essential Question in your text, journal, and On Assignment at myWorldGeography.com. Use what you've learned to write an essay about the challenges of diversity in ancient or medieval Europe.

Workshop Skill: Understand the Four Types of Essays

First you must decide what type of essay you want to write. There are four essay types: narrative, expository, research, and persuasive.

Narrative Essay This essay is similar to a story. It has characters, a setting, and a plot.
- The characters are the people that the story is about, and the setting is the time and place in which the story happens.
- The plot is the sequence of events that take place. Plots include conflict and lead up to a climax, which is the turning point of the story.

Expository Essay This essay has a main idea supported by evidence and examples.
- An introductory paragraph opens with a thesis sentence that states the main idea.
- The introduction is followed by body paragraphs. Each one discusses a point that supports the main idea. Evidence and examples show that the supporting points are true.
- The conclusion sums up the essay by restating the thesis and supporting points.

Research Essay This essay has the same structure as an expository essay. The difference lies in the type of evidence used to prove supporting points.
- Evidence and examples should come from a broad range of reliable sources.
- Writers use quotations, footnotes, and a bibliography to show where they located the evidence used in the essay.

Persuasive Essay This essay is written when the author wants to convince readers to adopt an opinion or take action.
- The introduction tells why the topic is important. Then the thesis statement explains what the writer wants readers to think or do.
- In the body paragraphs, the writer uses both arguments and evidence to prove the supporting points.
- The conclusion reviews the main points and urges the reader to adopt the opinion or take the action mentioned.

Identify Essay Types Use what you have learned to identify the different essay types. Read the four descriptions in the table on the next page. In the column on the right, write if the essay described is a narrative, expository, research, or persuasive one.

Essay Description	Type
1. The essay urges people of different cultures to stop fighting and learn from each other. It offers examples of people who have gained new insights from other cultures.	__________
2. The essay examines whether nations with diverse populations develop more new inventions than those nations who have people who conform. It contains graphs, charts, statistics, and quotations. Sources are listed in footnotes.	__________
3. The essay states that education helps people learn to understand other cultures. It explains three general ways that this can occur.	__________
4. The essay tells a story about a neighborhood in which ethnic groups fight because of conflicting customs. The story ends when two neighbors reach a compromise.	__________

Plan Your Essay

Use the following questions to help you make some decisions about your essay.

(1) What do I want to say about the challenges of diversity in ancient or medieval Europe?

____

____

(2) Do I want to tell a story, explain an idea, present evidence, or persuade others about something?

____

____

(3) What type of essay will best help me accomplish my goal?

____

____

Organize Your Essay

Now that you have decided on an essay type, outline your essay. Remember to have an introductory paragraph, three body paragraphs, and a conclusion. Review how to structure each of those paragraphs. Then create your outline.

Draft Your Essay

Write your essay using the outline you created. When you're done, proofread your essay.

Essential Question

What makes a nation?

Preview Before you begin this chapter, think about the Essential Question. Understanding how the Essential Question connects to your life will help you understand the chapter you are about to read.

Connect to Your Life

1 Think about foreign nations that you have visited, read about, or seen in TV shows and movies. What makes those nations different from the United States?

Things That Make Nations Different From Each Other			
Institutions	• Geography	• Culture	• Other

Connect to the Chapter

2 Suppose you are going to start a new nation. What are the essential things that your nation would need? Before you read the chapter, flip through every page and note the red headings, maps, and other pictures. Use your preview of the chapter to consider what you would need and record your ideas on the concept web.

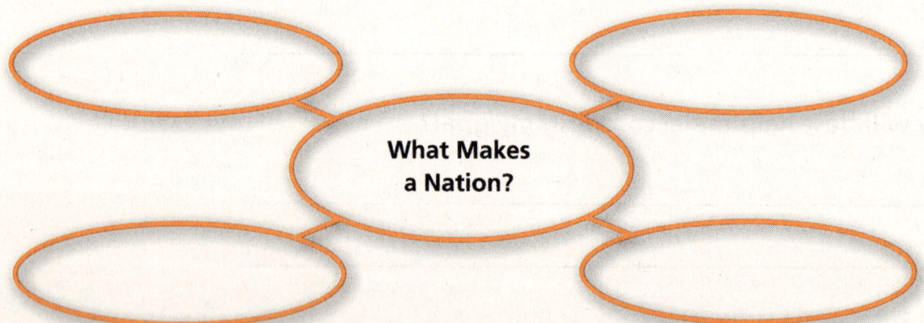

3 Now predict the ways that European countries have defined and expressed their nationhood. Record your ideas on the concept web using a different color pen or pencil.

4 After reading the chapter, return to this page. Were your predictions accurate? Why or why not?

____

____

 ____

Name _________________________ Class _________________________ Date ___________

Connect to myStory: The Battle of the Spanish Armada

(1) Write a brief summary of the story about Elizabeth I and the Spanish Armada.

____

____

(2) Record the main events of the story on the cause-and-effect chart below.

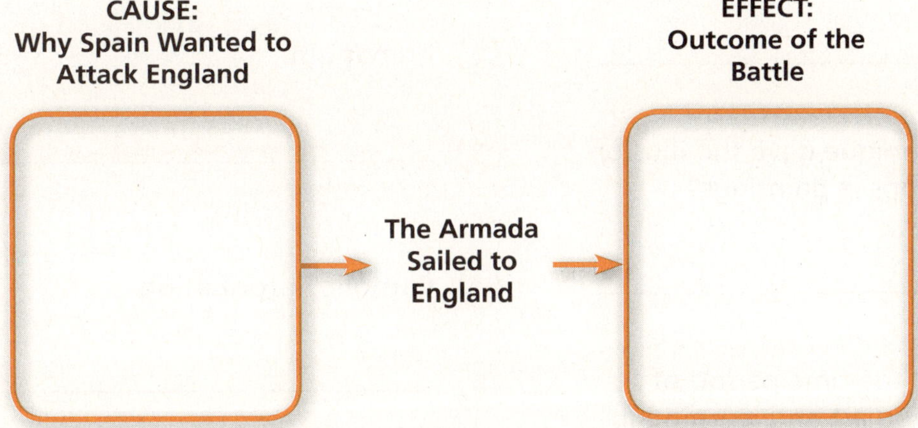

(3) What do you think was the long-term impact of England's victory? Explain.

____

____

____

Word Wise

Vocabulary Quiz Show Some quiz shows a question and expect the contestant to give the answer. In other shows the contestant is given an answer and must supply the question. If the blank is in the question column, write the question that would result in the answer in the answer column. If the answer is supplied, write the appropriate question.

QUESTION

1. What do you call the movement that led to the formation of Protestant churches?

2. _________________________

3. What artistic technique gave the illusion of three dimensions in paintings?

4. _________________________

5. What do you call the time period of renewed interest in art and learning in Europe?

ANSWER

1. _________________________

2. humanism

3. _________________________

4. Catholic Reformation

5. _________________________

Name _________________________ Class _________________________ Date ___________

Take Notes

Map Skills Use the maps in *all* sections of this chapter to make a key and to label the Places to Know on the outline map below. Remember, in addition to this section, you will need to refer to Sections 2 through 5.

Places to Know!

Countries		• Cities
England	Poland	• Wittenberg
Scotland	Romania	• Paris
Sweden	Belgium	• London
Spain		• Constantinople
Italy		• Berlin

Essential Question

How might a desire to build a stronger nation affect a ruler's decision to become a Protestant or a Catholic?

____

____

____

Word Wise

Sentence Builder Complete the sentences using the information you learned in this section. Include terminal punctuation.

(1) **Absolutism** allowed European kings _______________________

____

(2) The **caravel** helped the Portuguese _______________________

____

(3) On the Spanish **plantations**, which were _______________________,

farmers _______________________

____

(4) The **triangular trade** was _______________________

____

(5) Advances in **cartography** led to _______________________

____

(6) _______________________ searched for the **Northwest Passage**

because _______________________

____

Name _______________________ Class _______________________ Date _______________________

Take Notes

Sequence Record events from the history of Europe on the timeline below.

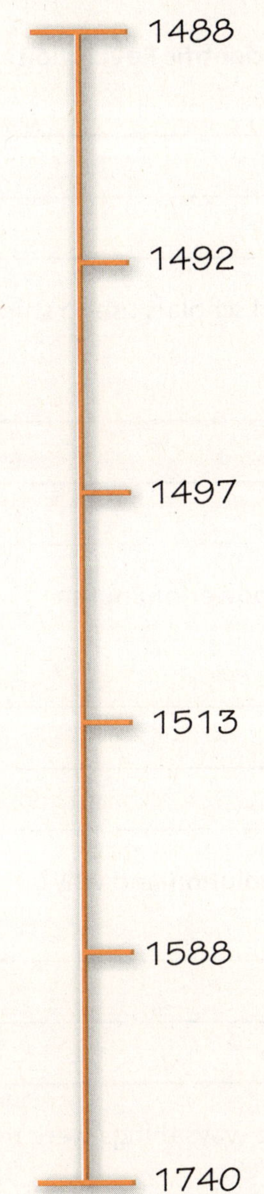

Essential Question

How might wars among European powers have helped build loyalty to the new nation-states?

____

____

____

Word Wise

Words In Context For each question below, write an answer that shows your understanding of the boldfaced key term.

① What major changes took place during the **Scientific Revolution**?

____

____

____

② During the **Enlightenment**, what methods did scholars use to study human nature?

____

____

____

③ How did the **English Bill of Rights** affect the power of English monarchs?

____

____

____

④ What event led to the start of the **French Revolution** and why?

____

____

____

⑤ During the **Industrial Revolution**, how did the ways things were made change?

____

____

____

Name _______________________________ Class ___________________ Date ____________

Take Notes

Cause and Effect Use the graphic organizer below to record the causes and effects of the Scientific Revolution, the French Revolution, and the Industrial Revolution.

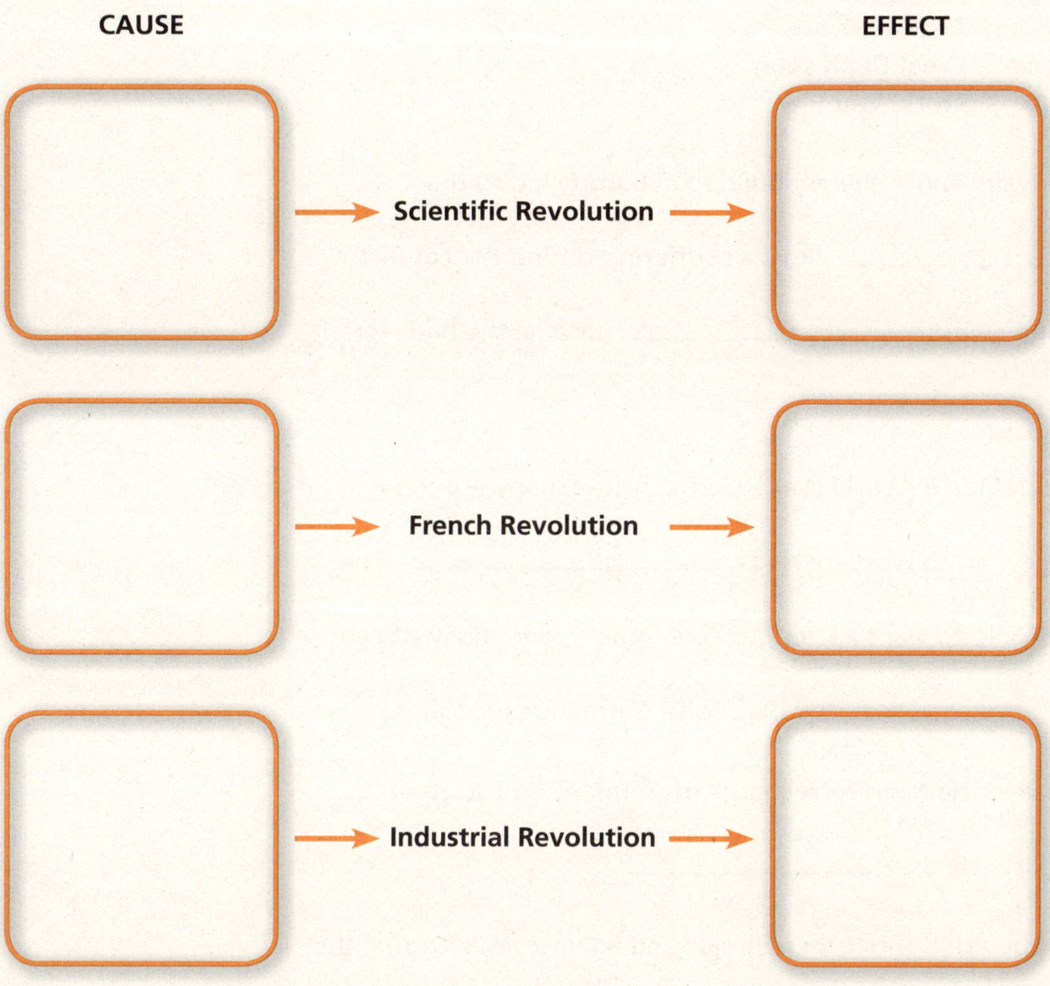

Essential Question

How did the Napoleonic Wars encourage nationalistic feelings in Europe?

____

____

____

Name _________________________________ Class _____________________________ Date ___________

Word Wise

Word Bank Choose one word from the word bank to fill in each blank.
When you have finished, you will have a short summary of important ideas
from the section.

Word Bank

communism	fascism
Holocaust	Great Depression
World War I	World War II

Nationalistic rivalry and a military buildup in Europe led to the

outbreak of _____________________. Russia's suffering during the conflict

caused a revolution in which _____________________ became the basis for

the new government.

After being defeated in World War I, Germany had many economic

problems, which grew much worse during the _____________________. The

problems caused people to want a stronger government, and many citizens

thought that _____________________ would solve Germany's problems.

A political party called the Nazis took charge of Germany and started

another huge conflict called _____________________.

The Nazis, led by Adolf Hitler, were prejudiced against Jews. During the

war, the Nazis tried to eliminate all European Jews in a program of mass

murder called the _____________________. For the second time in 30 years,

the Allies defeated Germany in a global war.

Name ____________________________ Class __________________ Date ___________

Take Notes

Compare and Contrast In this section, you read about two world wars.
Use the Venn diagram below to describe their similarities and differences.

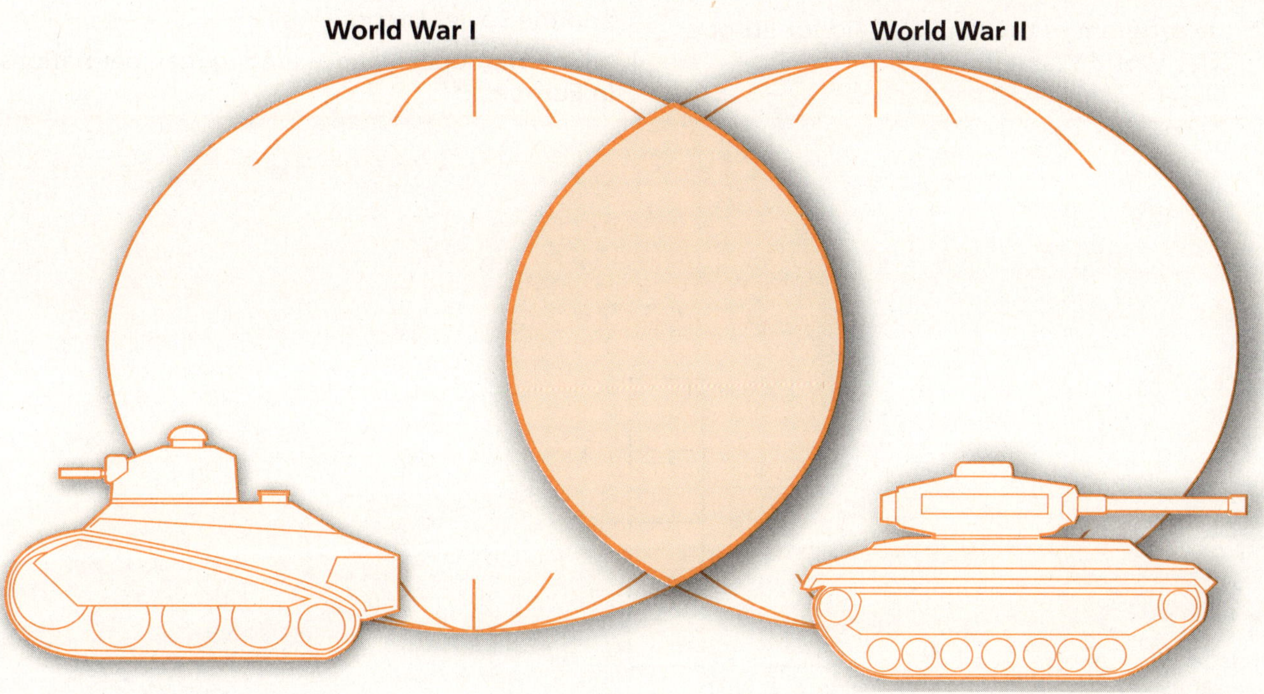

Essential Question

Why did so many nations gain independence after World War I?

____

____

____

Name _______________________________ Class _______________________________ Date ___________

Word Wise

Crossword Puzzle The clues describe key terms from this section. Fill in the numbered *Across* boxes with the correct key terms. Then, do the same with the *Down* clues.

Across	Down
1. its removal reunited Germany 2. the program of U.S. financial aid for Europe after World War II	3. a period of hostility between the United States and the Soviet Union 4. an international alliance among member nations in Europe

Name ________________________ Class ____________________ Date ___________

Take Notes

Main Ideas and Details Use what you have read in this section about Europe to complete the chart below. First, find the topic heading in the chapter. Write its main idea in your own words. Then give two details that support it.

Topic: Cold War and Division

Main idea:

Details:

1.

2.

Topic: The European Union

Main idea:

Details:

1.

2.

Topic: Democracy Spreads East

Main idea:

Details:

1.

2.

Topic: Europe Faces Challenges

Main idea:

Details:

1.

2.

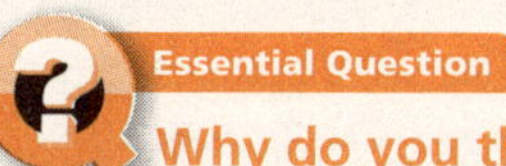

Essential Question

Why do you think East and West Germans still felt that they belonged to a single nation after more than 40 years apart?

____

____

____

Prepare to Write

Throughout this chapter, you have explored the Essential Question in your text, journal, and On Assignment at myWorldGeography.com. Use these notes and what you have learned about Europe to write an essay detailing the elements that form a nation.

Workshop Skill: Use the Writing Process

Writing is a process with four different steps. However, it is not a linear process like baking a cake. You do not always have to do the steps in the same order or completely finish each step before starting the next. In writing, you can go back to earlier steps and do them over or add to what you did before. The four steps of the writing process are:

Prewrite Decide on a topic, brainstorm, gather information, take notes, and make an outline. While this is the first step, it is also one you may frequently revisit. When you are in the middle of drafting or revising, you may realize that you need to do more research.

Draft Working from your prewriting notes and outline, write the first draft of the essay. At this stage, you put your ideas into sentences and paragraphs. Remember that each paragraph needs a main idea expressed in a topic sentence. Other sentences support and explain that main idea. Use transitions to connect sentences within paragraphs and to show links between paragraphs.

Revise Reread your piece, looking for ways to improve the writing. Your goal is to make it as clear as possible. Make sure you have explained all your ideas completely. Ask yourself these questions: *Is the essay organized in the best way? Are the sentences too wordy?* Also, be sure you have used accurate nouns and active verbs. Be sure that your grammar and spelling are correct.

Present Prepare your final draft to share with others. Double space the manuscript. Include your name, the date, and the title of your piece. Again, proofread it carefully so that it is error free.

Prewrite

Let's practice the prewriting step. Review the notes you've taken and the assignments you've done related to the Essential Question, "What makes a nation?" Use the concept web below to brainstorm ideas.

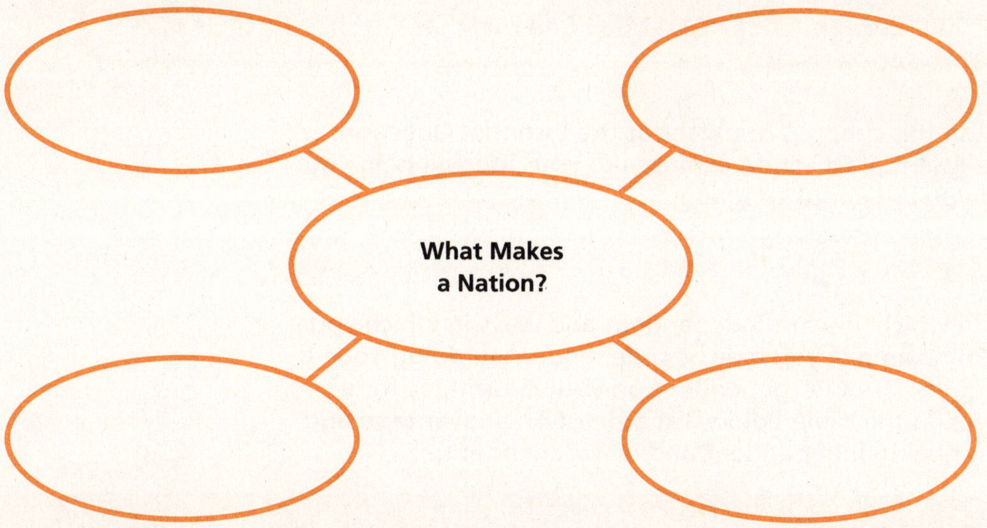

Create a Thesis Statement

Use the ideas from your concept web to write a thesis statement.

Thesis Statement ____

____

Your thesis statement needs three supporting ideas:

1. ____

2. ____

3. ____

Draft Your Essay

Use the information you brainstormed above to write your essay on another piece of paper. You should have five paragraphs: an introduction, three body paragraphs, and a conclusion. Follow the steps in the writing process to revise, edit, and present your essay.

Name _________________________ Class _________________ Date __________

Is it better to be independent or interdependent?

Preview Before you begin this chapter, think about the Essential Question. Understanding how the Essential Question connects to your life will help you understand the chapter you are about to read.

Connect to Your Life

1. Think about ways in which you are independent and ways in which you rely upon others. For example, you may be independent in doing your chores at home, but you are interdependent on your classmates for a school group project. In the table below, list at least one advantage and one disadvantage of being independent and interdependent.

	Advantages	Disadvantages
Independent		
Interdependent		

2. Think of a situation in which you might act alone for part of the time and act with a group for part of the time. What are the advantages of combining independence and interdependence?

____

____

Connect to the Chapter

3. Before you read the chapter, flip through every page. Note the boldfaced headings, maps, and other pictures. Try to predict areas in which European nations act independently and areas in which they act together. Record your predictions in the Venn diagram below.

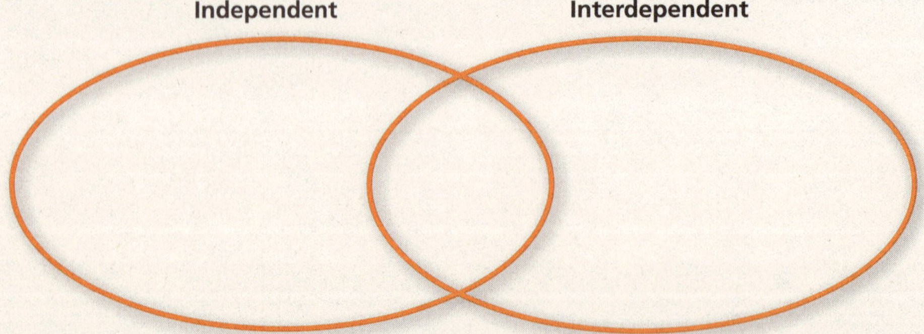

4. After reading the chapter, circle your predictions that were accurate.

Name _______________________________ Class ___________________________ Date ____________

Connect to myStory: Europe at Her Doorstep

1 In the table below, list the different cultures that are part of Yasmin's background. Then list details about how each culture influences her daily life.

Culture	How It Influences Yasmin

2 How was Yasmin's family affected by Sweden's decision to join the European Union?

____

____

3 How do you think other Europeans have been affected by their country's membership in the European Union? Write your predictions below.

____

____

____

Word Wise

Vocabulary Quiz Show Some quiz shows ask a question and expect the contestant to give the answer. In other shows, the contestant is given an answer and must supply the question. If the blank is in the question column, write the question that would result in the answer given. If the question is supplied, write the appropriate answer.

QUESTION	ANSWER
1 What is the source of the streams that flow from the Alps?	**1** _______________________________
2 _______________________________	**2** peninsula
3 What type of flat or gently rolling landform stretches across much of Western Europe?	**3** _______________________________
4 _______________________________	**4** tundra
5 What is the name for the thick forest of coniferous trees in Northern Europe?	**5** _______________________________
6 _______________________________	**6** pollution
7 What is the word for Europe's rich soil made of sediments deposited by glaciers?	**7** _______________________________

Name _______________________ Class _______________________ Date ___________

Take Notes

Map Skills Use the maps in your book to make a key and to label the Places to Know the outline map below.

Places to Know!

Countries	City	Physical Features
France	London	Alps
Greece		Iberian Peninsula
Italy		North Sea
Iceland		Mediterranean Sea

Essential Question

Look at the languages map in this section. Do you think the number of languages spoken by EU members helps or harms Western Europe?

____

____

____

Name _______________________________ Class _____________________ Date ___________

Word Wise

Word Bank Choose one word from the word bank to fill in each blank. When you have finished, you will have a short summary of important ideas from the section.

Word Bank

constitutional monarchy   gross domestic product (GDP)
cultural borrowing   Parliament
cradle-to-grave system

The United Kingdom has a queen, but the _____________________

actually makes all the laws. Since the government is a

_____________________, the queen is just a ceremonial leader. The prime

minister is the real political leader of the nation.

Scandinavian countries have a _____________________ in which the

governments provide benefits for people of all ages. Scandinavia is so far

north that in the summer it has a period of almost 24-hour sunlight called

the white nights season.

The United Kingdom, Ireland, and the Scandinavian countries have all

experienced increasing numbers of immigrants, which leads to

_____________________. The countries in these regions are generally

economically prosperous. They have a high _____________________, which is

the total value of all goods and services produced and sold in a nation in one

year. A country with a high GDP often has a good standard of living for most

of its citizens.

Name ________________________________   Class ____________________   Date ____________

Take Notes

Compare and Contrast In this section, you read about the United Kingdom and the countries of Scandinavia. Use the Venn diagram below to describe how they are similar and how they differ.

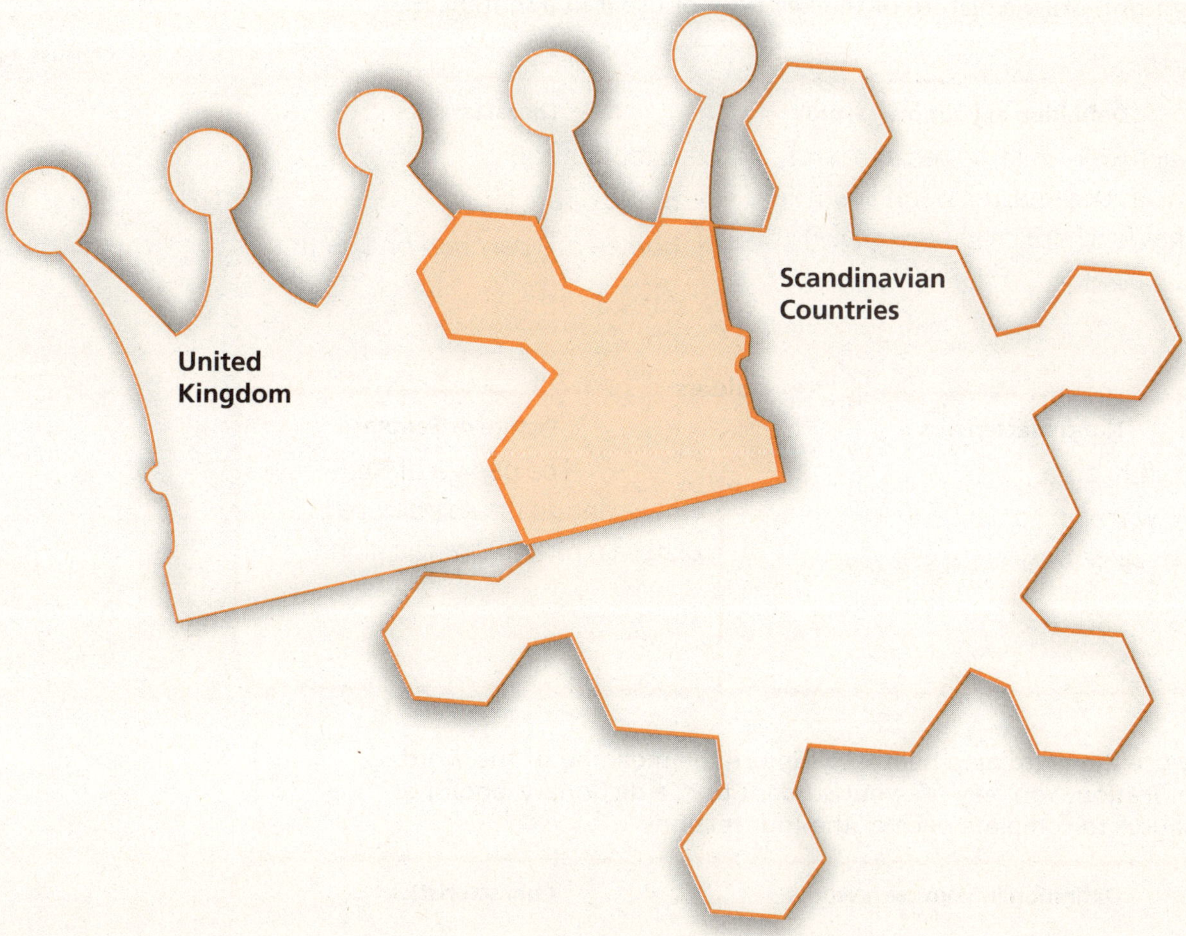

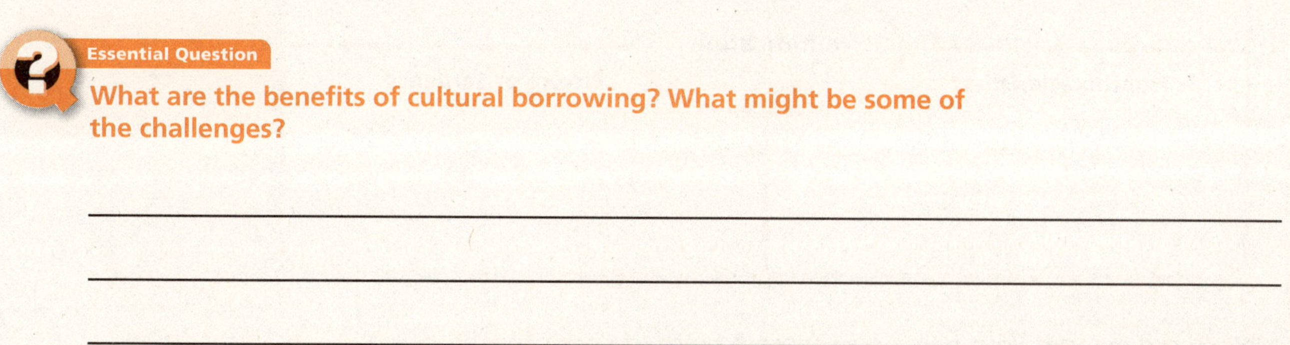

Essential Question

What are the benefits of cultural borrowing? What might be some of the challenges?

____

____

____

Word Wise

Word Map Follow the model below to make a word map. The key term *polders* is in the center oval. Write the definition in your own words at the upper left. In the upper right, list Characteristics, which means words or phrases that relate to the term. At the lower left list Noncharacteristics, which means words and phrases that would not be associated with it. In the lower right, draw a picture of the key term or use it in a sentence.

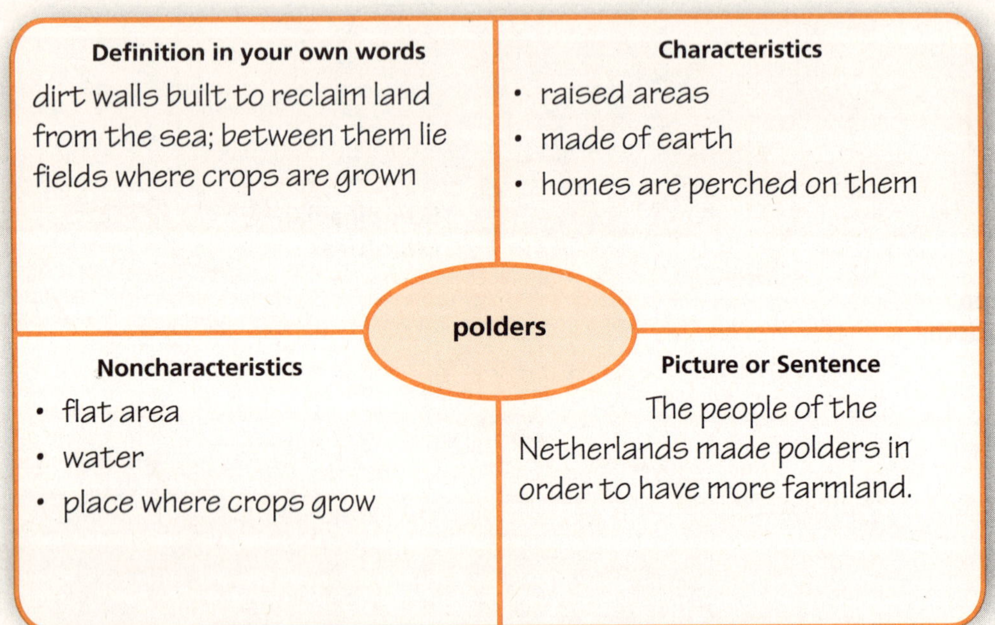

Now use the word map below to explore the meaning of the word *reunification*. You may use your student text, a dictionary, and/or a thesaurus to complete each of the four sections.

Make word maps of your own on a separate piece of paper for the following words: *privatization* and *gross national product (GNP)*.

Name ________________________________ Class ____________________ Date __________

Take Notes

Main Ideas and Details In this section, you read about the countries of West Central Europe. Use the concept web below to record main ideas and details about the region's culture and international partnerships.

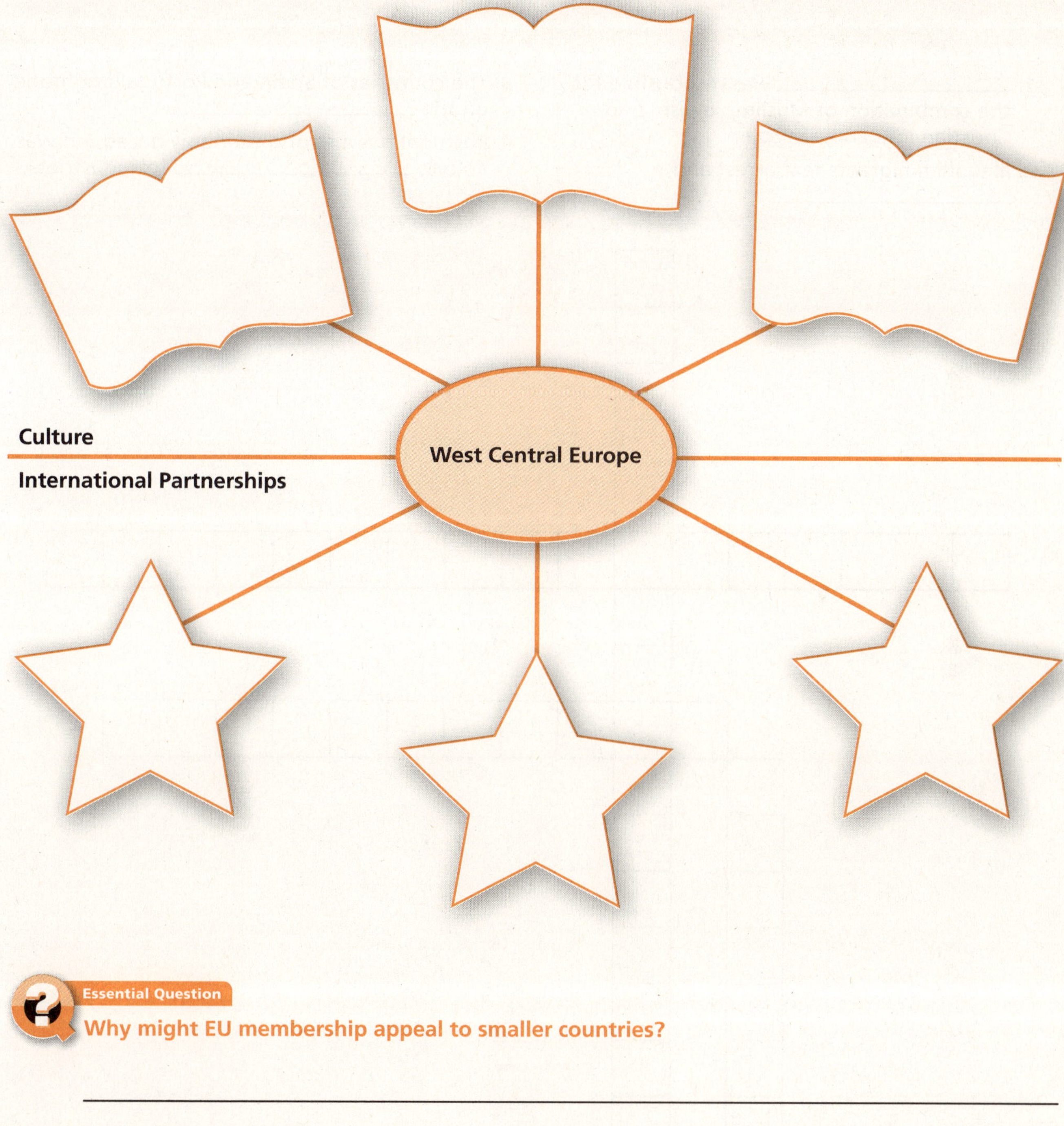

Why might EU membership appeal to smaller countries?

____

____

____

Name _______________________________ Class _____________________ Date ___________

Word Wise

Crossword Puzzle The clues describe key terms from this section. Fill in the numbered *Across* boxes with the correct key terms. Then, do the same with the *Down* clues.

Across

1. _____________________ was responsible for the combination of Muslim, Jewish, and Christian influences in Spain.

2. Illegal immigrants fear arrest and _____________________.

Down

3. The countries of Spain and Portugal are found on the _____________________.

4. Portugal has a strong economy because it was able to _____________________ its industries.

Name _______________________________ Class _____________________________ Date ______________

Take Notes

Cause and Effect In this section, you read about Greece, Italy, Portugal, and Spain. Use the flowchart below to record the causes and effects of economic change and immigration in Southern Europe.

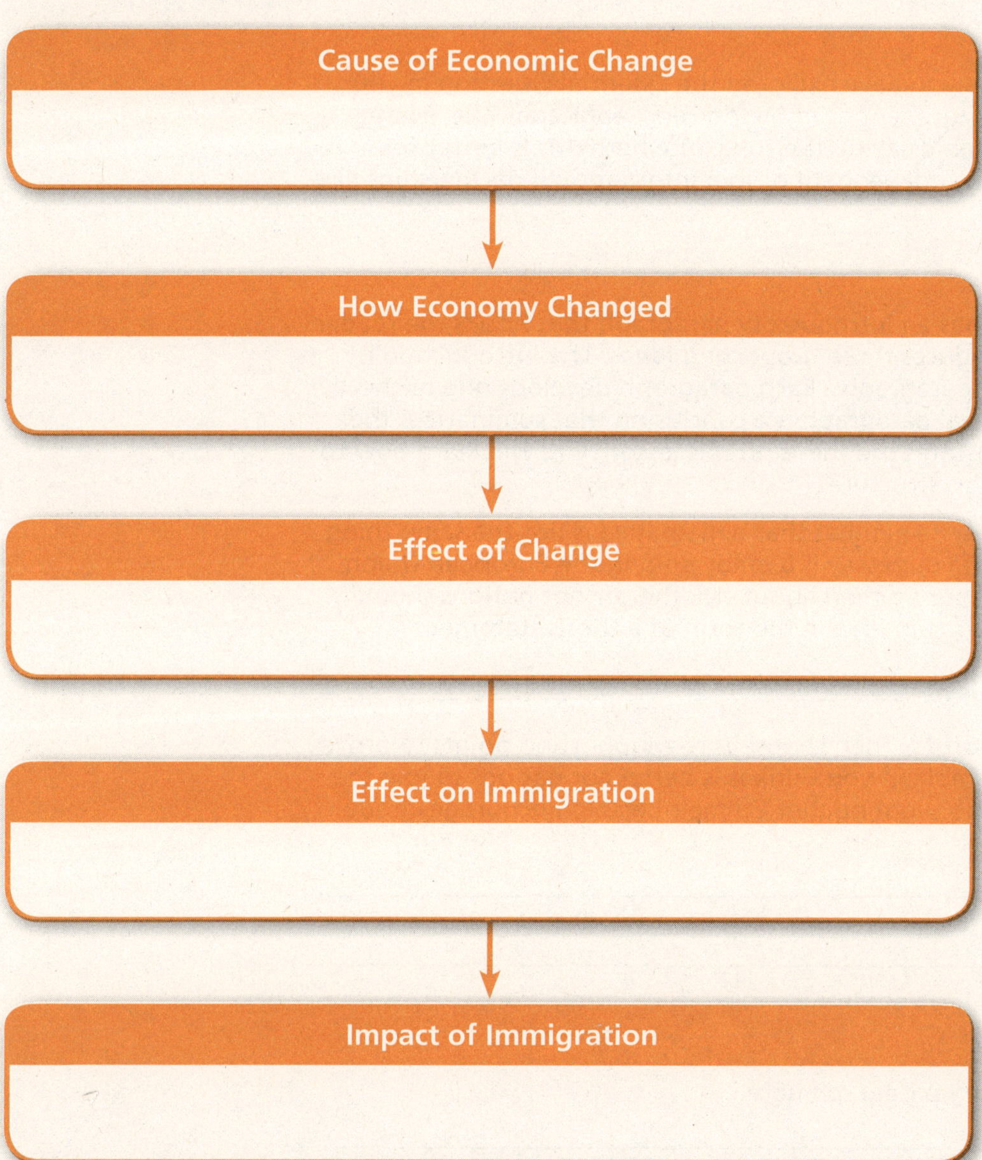

Essential Question

Has the European Union helped Southern Europe? Explain why or why not.

____

____

____

Is it better to be independent or interdependent?

Prepare to Write

Throughout this chapter, you have explored the Essential Question in your text, journal, and On Assignment at myWorldGeography.com. Use what you've learned to write an essay on the topic of whether it is better for European nations to stay independent or join international partnerships like the European Union.

Workshop Skill: Outline An Essay

A five-paragraph essay has an introductory paragraph that hooks the reader, states a thesis, and introduces three supporting ideas. The introduction is followed by three body paragraphs. Each paragraph develops one of the supporting ideas. The final paragraph is a conclusion that summarizes the supporting ideas and restates the thesis. In this lesson, you will learn how to outline an essay using this structure.

Identify the Main Idea Remember that a main idea is not the same thing as the topic. The topic of your essay is membership in the European Union. Your main idea will be your *opinion* about whether or not nations should join the EU. Express your main idea in the form of a thesis statement.

Write a Thesis Statement ____

Choose Supporting Points Then choose three supporting points to prove your statement. For example, if you think it is better for nations to join the EU, one supporting point might be that EU membership encourages trade.

____

____

Outline the Introductory Paragraph

Outline your introductory paragraph here:

Hook ____

Thesis Statement ____

Sentence Summarizing the Supporting Ideas _____________________

Outline Body Paragraphs

Each paragraph needs a topic sentence that states the main idea. Include evidence to support the main idea. End the paragraph with a concluding sentence that tells how the information supports your thesis statement.

Body Paragraph 1
Topic sentence

____

____

Supporting detail

____

____

Supporting detail(s)

____

____

Concluding sentence

____

____

Follow this format to write two more body paragraphs.

Outline Your Conclusion

In the conclusion, you review your thesis, summarize your supporting points, explain how those points proved your statement, and end by telling the reader why this topic matters.

Paragraph 5: Conclusion

Restate the Thesis ____________________________________

Summary of Supporting Points ____________________________

What the Supporting Points Prove ___________________________

Why the Topic Matters _________________________________

Draft Your Essay

Write your essay on your own paper. When you have finished, proofread it with a partner.

Name ___________________________ Class ___________________ Date ___________

How can you measure success?

Preview Before you begin this chapter, think about the Essential Question. Understanding how the Essential Question connects to your life will help you understand the chapter you are about to read.

Connect to Your Life

(1) What does success mean to you? Think of some ways to measure success in the categories shown in the table below. List at least one way in each column. For example, under sports, you could list winning a major game in your favorite sport.

Measures of Personal Success			
Sports	Arts & Drama	Hobbies	Relationships

(2) Think about what it takes to achieve success. Is it more difficult to reach some goals than others? Does this change the value of the success?

____

____

Connect to the Chapter

(3) Before you read the chapter, flip through every page and note the red headings, maps, and pictures. What factors might limit success in Eastern Europe? What factors might encourage success? Use two different colored pens or pencils to list these factors on the table below.

Measures of National Success			
Economy	Politics	Social Services	Environment

(4) Read the chapter. Review the predictions you made in the table above. Circle the ones that were correct.

Name _________________________________ Class _____________________________ Date ____________

Connect to myStory: Serhiy's Leap

1 Think about ways that your life is like Serhiy's life. What challenges
does your family face daily? How does school play a role in your life?
What are your hopes for the future?

____

____

2 Use this Venn diagram to compare your life with Serhiy's life. Think
about family challenges, school, and hopes for the future.

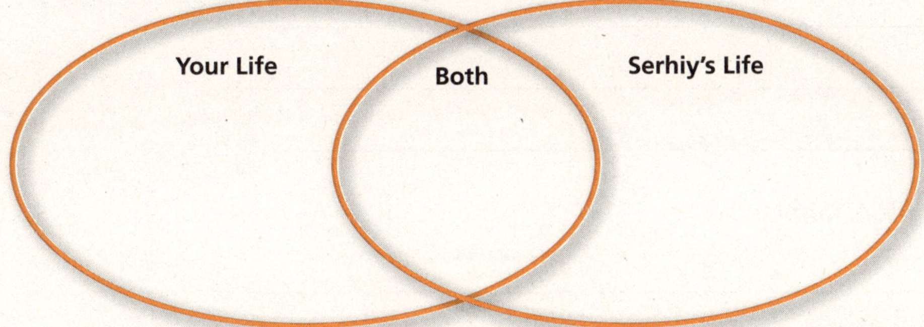

3 In the table below, list the challenges Serhiy faces as he tries to help his
family meet its goals.

Daily Life	Making a Living	Getting an Education

4 How do you think these challenges are affecting the people and
nations of Eastern Europe?

____

____

____

Word Wise

Words In Context For each question below, write an answer that shows your understanding of the boldfaced key term.

1 Why have so many Eastern European Jews chosen to **emigrate**?

____

____

____

2 What happens during an **ice age**?

____

____

____

3 How can **acid rain** affect farmland?

____

____

____

4 What kind of land is best for **mechanized farming** and why?

____

____

____

Name _________________________ Class _________________________ Date _____________

Take Notes

Map Skills Use the maps in your book to make a key and to label the Places to Know on the outline map below.

Places to Know!

Physical Features	Bodies of Water	Countries
Balkan Mountains	Black Sea	Poland
North European Plain	Baltic Sea	Ukraine
Great Hungarian Plain	Danube River	Bosnia
		Herzegovina

Essential Question

To join the European Union, countries must meet certain environmental standards. Do you think protecting the environment should be one measure of a country's success? Why or why not?

____

____

____

Word Wise

Vocabulary Quiz Show Some quiz shows ask a question and expect the contestant to give the answer. In other shows, the contestant is given an answer and must supply the question. If the blank is in the question column, write the question that would result in the answer given. If the question is supplied, write the appropriate answer.

QUESTION	ANSWER
(1) What do you call a person who sets up and manages his or her own business?	(1) _______________________
(2) _______________________	(2) ethnic cleansing
(3) If one part of a country breaks away from that country and declares itself a new nation, what is that action called?	(3) _______________________
(4) _______________________	(4) capital
(5) What is the word for a specific style of food?	(5) _______________________

Name _______________________________   Class ___________________________   Date _____________

Take Notes

Compare and Contrast In this section, you read how different countries and parts of Eastern Europe have succeeded, while others have faced challenges. In the table below, record the successes and the challenges in each section of Eastern Europe.

	Successes	Challenges
Poland and the Baltic Nations		
Central Europe		
The Balkan Nations		
Ukraine, Belarus, and Moldova		

Essential Question

Give an example of one Eastern European nation that has been successful in recent years. Why do you think this country has been successful?

____

____

____

____

How can you measure success?

Prepare to Write

Throughout this chapter, you have explored the Essential Question in your text, journal, and On Assignment at myWorldGeography.com. Use what you've learned to write a compare and contrast essay about how any two countries in the region have changed since the fall of the Soviet Union. Consider how each of these factors has influenced each nation's progress: physical geography and natural resources; ethnic groups; conflict/war; economic goals; and government actions.

Workshop Skill: Write an Introduction and Thesis Statement

In this lesson, you will learn more about developing a thesis and introduction for your essay. A thesis is the main point you want to make in your essay. It is neither a topic nor a title. It is an idea that you will explain in the essay. Writers generally state their thesis in the introduction. Why? The first paragraph is like an outline to your essay. It tells readers your main point and briefly lists the arguments you will make to support it.

Determine the Essay Type Think about the characteristics of the type of essay you will write. Look for signal words in the essay question. For example, the words *compare and contrast* tell you that your essay must identify and explain ways in which two countries are similar and different. This means you must give facts about both countries and then explain how the information is related.

Write a Thesis Statement Consider the main point you want to make in your essay and phrase it as a thesis statement. Here's an example: *After achieving independence from the Soviet Union, the Czech Republic had more success than Slovakia.* This statement is specific to the question and mentions two nations: the Czech Republic and Slovakia. The rest of the essay will describe the success of the Czech Republic and the success of Slovakia, discussing reasons for the different outcomes the two nations have achieved. The thesis statement may appear at the start or at the end of your introduction.

Build the Introduction An introduction tells readers what your essay will be about and why they should care about the topic. Thus, you must give readers a little background. For example, you might explain that Czechoslovakia was controlled by the Soviet Union until 1990. In 1993 it split into the Czech Republic and Slovakia. Briefly state the main points the whole essay will make. You might choose to do this with one sentence describing the overall success of one nation and then another sentence explaining the success of the other nation. Finally, tell your readers why the topic is important.

Revise Your Thesis as You Write Sometimes as you explain your arguments, you may find that they don't exactly support the thesis. You may also change your topic a little bit. Keep checking and revising your thesis as you write. For example, in the sample thesis statement, you might replace *more success* with *success more quickly*. This adds a time element to the comparison.

As you revise your thesis, remember that it must:
- fit the essay assignment
- be clearly stated and easy to understand
- be supported by facts and logic

Here is a sample thesis and introduction:

Thesis *After becoming independent from the Soviet Union, the Czech Republic achieved success more quickly than Slovakia.*

Background *Until 1990, these two nations had been the Soviet-controlled nation called Czechoslovakia. They split into two separate nations in 1993.*

Main Point 1 *Historical circumstances favored the Czech Republic. The nation's leaders also increased their advantage with aggressive modernization policies.*

Main Point 2 *The Czech Republic had a diverse economy with many different industries which allowed for rapid modernization.*

Main Point 3 *Slovakia, however, had just one main industry. When that industry slowed, it hindered the modernization of the rest of the economy.*

Why it Matters *The history of these two countries since 1993 provides lessons about why countries struggle or succeed.*

Create Your Thesis and Introduction
Now write your own thesis and introduction.

Sample thesis ____

____

Background ____

____

Main Point 1 ____

____

Main Point 2 ____

____

Why it Matters ____

____

Draft Your Essay
Use the thesis and introduction in your essay, which will be written on another paper. Complete your essay, and proofread it with a partner.

Essential Question

What should governments do?

Preview Before you begin this chapter, think about the Essential Question. Understanding how the Essential Question connects to your life will help you understand the chapter you are about to read.

Connect to Your Life

1. Think of different ways in which the United States government affects your life. List at least one way in each column. For example, under laws you could list laws that prohibit stealing.

How the United States Government Affects My Life				
Laws	• Taxes	• Military	• Environment	• Transportation

2. Look at the table. Do you think the government should be doing everything you listed? Is there something that you think the government should do that it isn't doing? Write your ideas here.

____

Connect to the Chapter

3. Nations sometimes go through bad times such as wars or economic slowdowns. Do you think a government should take different actions during bad times than it does during good times? Record your ideas on the Venn diagram below.

What should governments do?

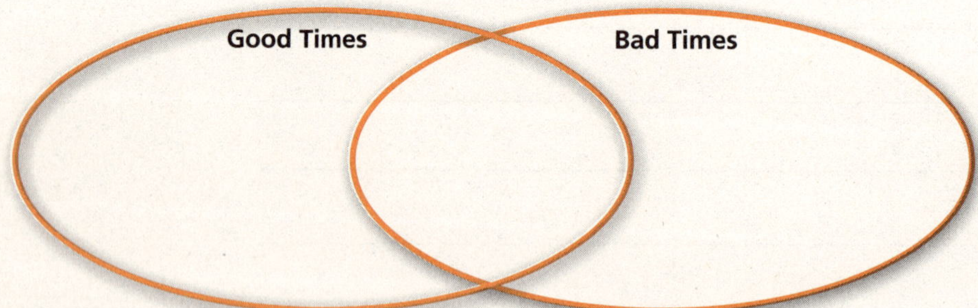

4. Before you read the chapter, flip through every page and note the red headings, maps, and other pictures. Now record your predictions of what actions the Russian government will take during bad times on the Venn diagram above using a different colored ink or pencil.

5. At the end of the chapter, come back to this page. Circle any accurate predictions you made.

Name _______________________ Class _______________________ Date ___________

Connect to myStory: Boris's Big Spin

① Fill in the table below to compare your life to Boris's life in each of the five areas listed.

How Our Lives Compare	My Life	Boris's Life
Family		
Travel		
Social Pressure		
Sports/Hobbies		
Military Conflict		

② Look at what you wrote in the table above. Tell one way in which your life is easier than Boris's. Explain.

____

____

____

③ Look at the table again. Tell one way in which your life is harder than Boris's. Explain.

____

____

____

④ What does Boris's story tell you about life in Russia today?

____

____

____

Word Wise

Word Bank Choose one word from the word bank to fill in each blank. When you have finished, you will have a short summary of important ideas from the section.

Word Bank

Ural Mountains	Siberia
Lake Baikal	steppes
permafrost	Kamchatka Peninsula

Russia is the largest nation on Earth; it stretches almost halfway around the globe! In fact, it lies on two continents: Europe and Asia. Although they are not very tall, the ___________________ separate Russia into European Russia and Asiatic Russia. Asiatic Russia is also called ___________________.

Russia has large grasslands, or ___________________, which is where its farmland is found. One of the challenges for Russia is that that much of its soil is ___________________, or permanently frozen soil beneath the tundra and taiga biomes. This makes constructing roads, railroads, and buildings difficult or even impossible.

Russia has some of the most interesting geographical features in the world. There are 160 volcanoes on Russia's ___________________, and 29 of them are active! The nation's huge ___________________ holds about 20 percent of Earth's freshwater. It contains more water than our five Great Lakes combined.

Name _______________________   Class _______________________   Date ___________

Take Notes

Map Skills Use the maps in your book to make a key and to label the Places to Know on the outline map below.

Essential Question

Look at the railroad mileage chart in this section. The Russian government helped pay the cost of building the Trans-Siberian Railroad. Why might governments invest in transportation systems?

____

____

____

Word Wise

Words in Context For each question below, write an answer that shows your understanding of the boldfaced key term.

1. What position did the **tsar** hold in the Russian government?

   ____

   ____

2. How did the **Kremlin** help demonstrate Russia's new standing in the world?

   ____

   ____

3. Why couldn't **serfs** move to the city?

   ____

   ____

4. Who were the **Bolsheviks**, and what did they do in the Russian Revolution?

   ____

   ____

5. In the name Soviet Union, what did **soviet** stand for?

   ____

   ____

6. How did Stalin's policy of **collectivization** change farming in the Soviet Union?

   ____

   ____

Name _________________________ Class _________________________ Date ___________

Take Notes

Cause and Effect Use the cause-and-effect boxes below to record information about the Russian Revolution and the fall of the Soviet Union.

RUSSIAN REVOLUTION

Causes:

Effects:

FALL OF SOVIET UNION

Causes:

Effects:

Essential Question

Think about the famines that have occurred throughout Russian history. What actions might a government take during disasters such as famines?

____

____

____

Word Wise

Vocabulary Quiz Show Some quiz shows ask a question and expect the contestant to give the answer. In other shows, the contestant is given an answer and must supply the question. If the blank is in the question column, write the question that would result in the answer given. If the question is supplied, write the appropriate answer.

QUESTION

1 _______________________

2 What do you call one of the most powerful nations on Earth?

3 _______________________

4 After people have paid taxes on their earnings, what is left over?

ANSWER

1 KGB

2 _______________________

3 censor

4 _______________________

Name _______________________________ Class _____________________ Date ____________

Take Notes

Main Ideas and Details In this section, you read about the many challenges faced by Russia today. Use the concept web below to record main ideas and details about those events.

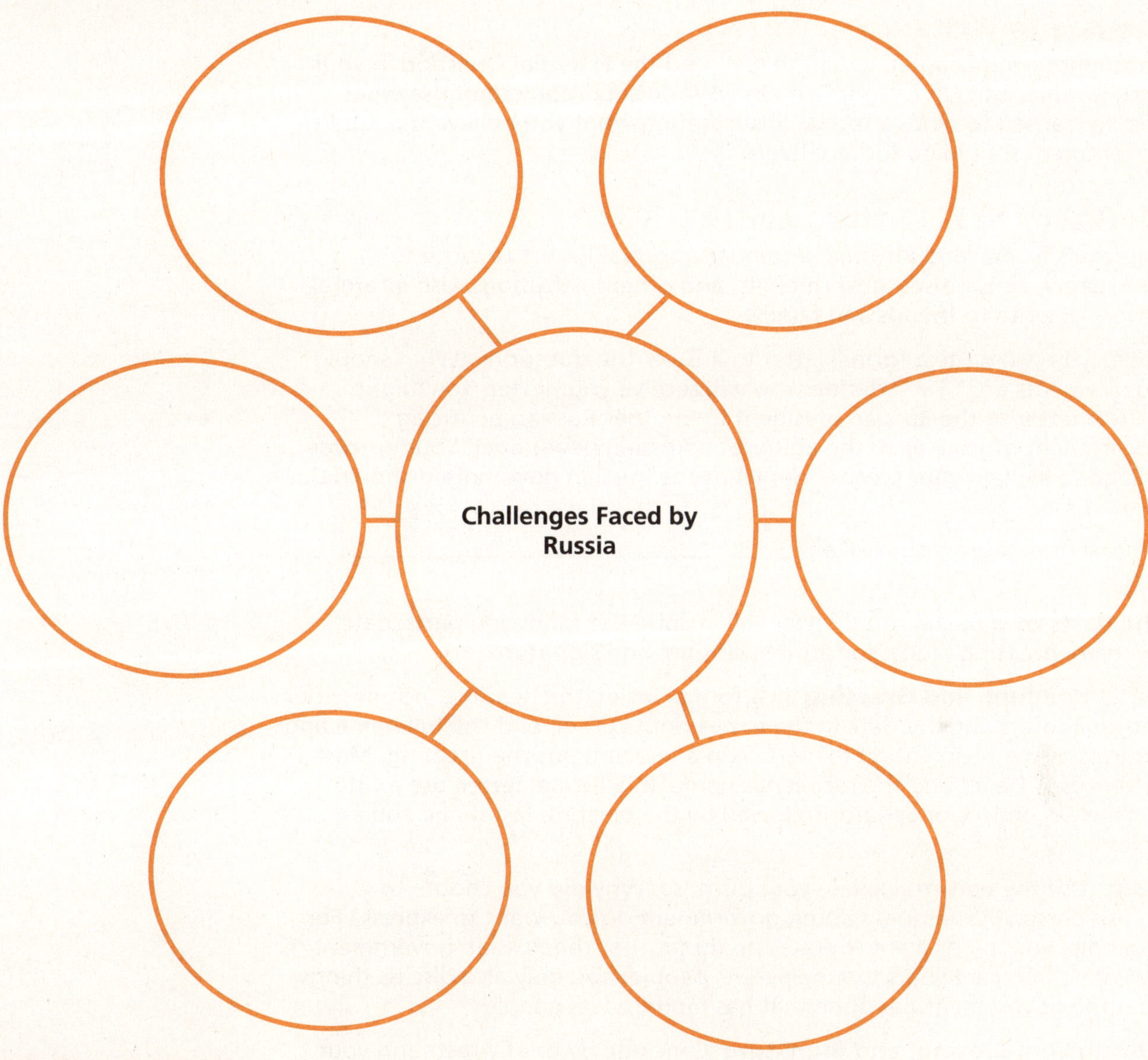

Essential Question

Think about the life expectancy and infant mortality graphs in this section. What do you think the government can do about the health problems in Russia?

____

____

____

What should governments do?

Prepare to Write

Throughout this chapter, you have explored the Essential Question in your text, journal, and On Assignment at myWorldGeography.com. Use what you've learned to write a formal letter stating what you believe the Russian government should do for its citizens.

Workshop Skill: Write a Letter

There are formal and informal letters. Use formal letters to write to newspapers, businesses, governments, and other institutions. Use informal letters to write to friends and family.

Today you will write a formal letter to answer the question, "What should governments do?" First, decide who will receive your letter. You might write a letter to the Russian president to another Russian politician or government official, or to the editor of a Russian newspaper. Your purpose will be to explain your ideas about what the Russian government should do.

Who will receive your letter? _________________________________

The Parts of a Letter Your letter will include the following parts: date, heading, greeting, body, conclusion, closing, and signature.

Date, Heading, and Greeting In a formal letter, the heading includes your return address and the date in the upper right corner, and the full name and address of the recipient on the left. Skip a line and put the greeting. Most letters use "Dear" and the recipient's name. In a formal letter, use a title such as *Dr.* or *Mrs.* or *Senator* followed by the person's last name and a colon.

Body Use the body to explain your purpose. Why did you choose to write to this person? What ideas about government do you want to express? For example, you might want to state the things that the Russian government has done in recent years that helped its people. You may also discuss things that the government has done that has hindered its people.

Conclusion, Closing, and Signature Conclude by briefly restating your main point. If you want the recipient to take action, such as working to pass a law or printing your letter in the newspaper, state that. Below the conclusion, skip a line, write a closing such as "Sincerely yours," or "Yours truly," followed by a comma. Sign your full name below it.

Draft Your Letter

Use the format below to write the first draft of your letter.

(your address and date; do not put your name) ______________________________

____

____

______________________________ **(name and address of recipient)**

____

____

____

Dear ____

Body ____

____

____

____

____

____

Conclusion ______________________________________

____

____

____

Closing ______________________________

Your signature ______________________________

Finalize Your Letter

Remember to follow the steps of the writing process to revise and edit your letter. Then neatly copy it onto a clean sheet of paper.

Who should benefit from a country's resources?

Preview Before you begin this chapter, think about the Essential Question. Understanding how the Essential Question connects to your life will help you understand the chapter you are about to read.

Connect to Your Life

1 How do you and your friends share? Think about sharing a bag of candy, taking turns playing a game, or sharing an object. What are the positives and negatives of different ways of sharing?

Different Ways to Share			
Sharing Strategy	Equal portion for all	Biggest appetite gets more	More for those who pay more	Other
Pros				
Cons				

Connect to the Chapter

2 Before you read the chapter, flip through every page. Note the headings, maps, and pictures. Then, predict how each of these sharing strategies might work when different countries try them.

____

____

3 Read the chapter. Think of how countries in West and Central Africa have shared resources in the ways shown in the chart below. Write yes or no in the first row. For those columns in which the answer is yes, write the name of the nation or group that used it in the second row.

Ways to Divide Resources in the Real World		
Sharing Strategy	Shares are based on need.	Wealthy and powerful people take more than others.	Everybody fights.
Used in West and Central Africa?			
Name (if yes)			

Name ________________________________ Class ____________________ Date __________

Connect to myStory:
A String of Dreams

(1) Think about a major store or a mall in your community. Where do the goods they sell come from? How do they get there?

____

____

____

(2) List five facts about Ghana that you learned from reading Evelyn's story.

Fact 1	Fact 2	Fact 3	Fact 4	Fact 5

(3) Based on Evelyn's story, predict if trade and commerce were important in the history of West and Central Africa. Do you think that trade and commerce have a major role in life there today? Why or why not?

____

____

____

Word Wise

Sentence Builder Complete the sentences using the information you learned in this section. Include terminal punctuation.

1 **Desertification** is one of the biggest worries in the **Sahel** because

____

____

2 On the African **savanna** the land is _____________________ and the

vegetation is ____

____

3 **Malaria** is a(n) _____________________ spread by _____________________

and is common in ____

____

4 **Deforestation** means _____________________ and is threatening to

cause **desertification** in the nations of _______________________________

____

5 A major problem threatening Africa is that **arable land** can become

____

Name _________________________   Class _________________   Date _________

Take Notes

Map Skills Use the maps in your book to make a key and to label the Places to Know on the outline map below.

Places to Know!

Cities	• Physical Features
Lagos	• Congo River
Kinshasa	• Niger River
Accra	•

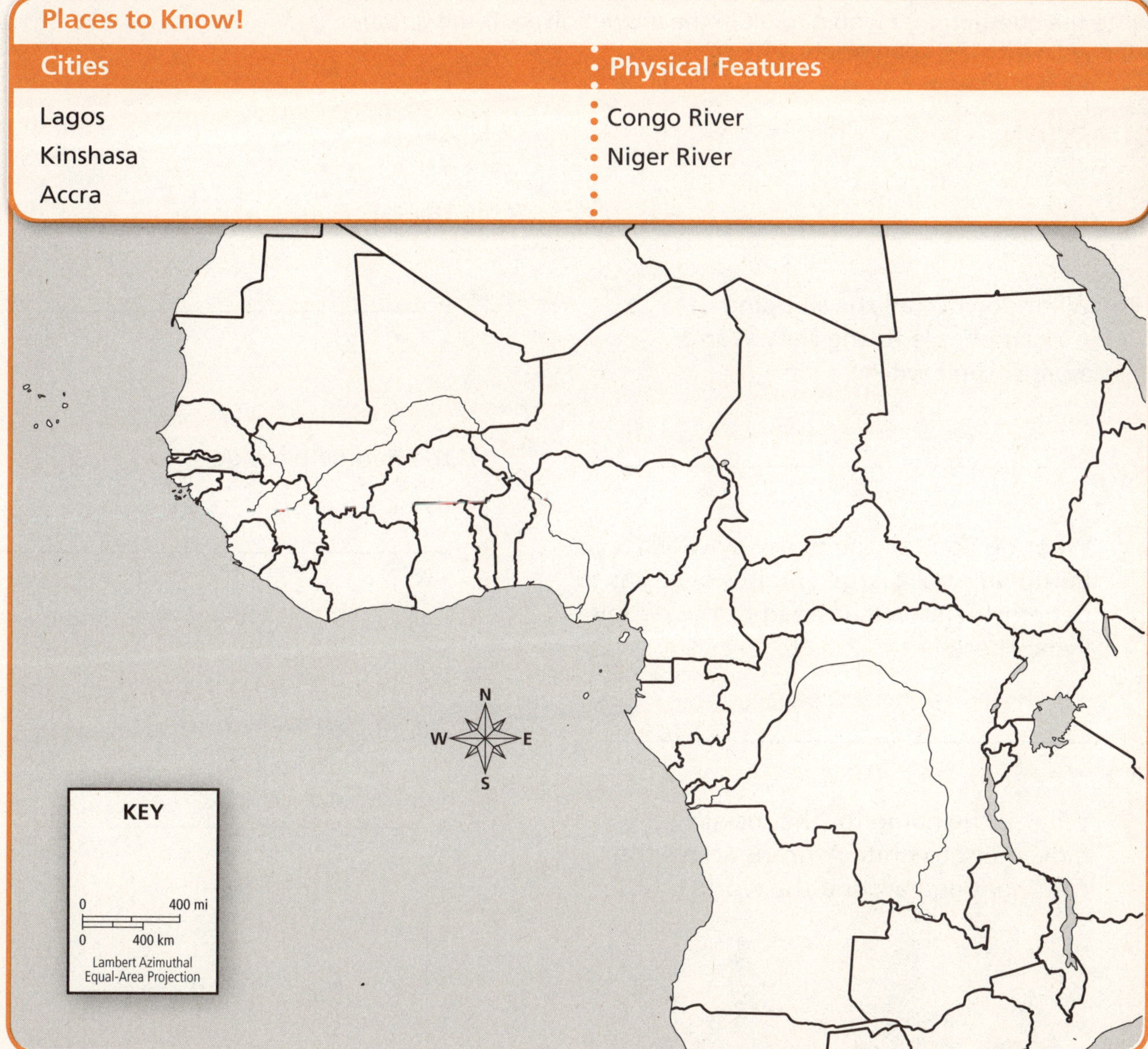

Essential Question

How might not having abundant farmland or natural resources affect a county?

____

____

Word Wise

Vocabulary Quiz Show Some quiz shows ask a question and expect the contestant to give the answer. In other shows, the contestant is given an answer and must supply the question. If the blank is in the question column, write the question that would result in the answer given. If the question is supplied, write the appropriate answer.

QUESTION	ANSWER
① _________________________	① the salt trade
② What do you call the shipping of African people to the New World against their will?	② _________________________
③ _________________________	③ the middle passage
④ What do you call the policy by which Europeans built large empires overseas to benefit themselves instead of the people living there?	④ _________________________
⑤ _________________________	⑤ colonialism
⑥ What is the name for the social movement to unite Africans across the continent and around the world?	⑥ _________________________

Name _______________________________ Class _______________________ Date ______________

Take Notes

Sequence Label each range of dates on the timeline with the event that happened or a state that existed in West and Central Africa during that period. Fill in two facts about each event or state.

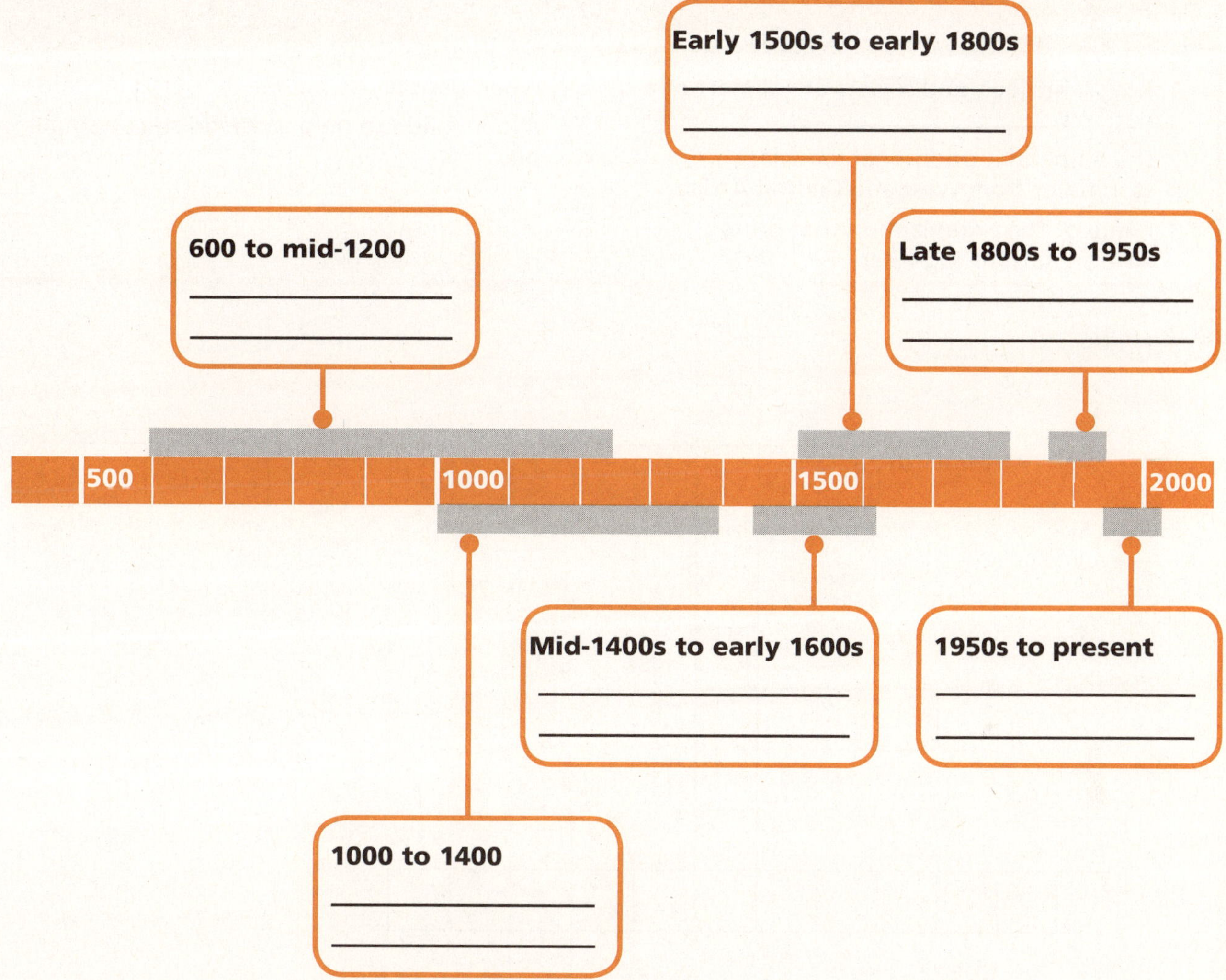

Essential Question

What role did natural resources play in the history of West and Central Africa?

____

____

____

Name _______________________________ Class ____________________ Date ___________

Word Wise

Crossword Puzzle The clues describe key terms from this section. Fill in the numbered *Across* boxes with the correct key terms. Then, do the same with the *Down* clues.

Across	Down
1. Roads, bridges, and sewers are all part of a nation's ______________.	4. when people use power for personal gain
2. the name of a traditional musician-storyteller from West and Central Africa	5. a loan made to help a person start a small business
3. name of the organization that brings African nations together	

Take Notes

Main Ideas and Details Use this table to help understand the main ideas of this section. Each box lists the name of a heading in this section. For each, write the main idea for that part and at least two supporting details about that main idea.

Economic Challenges	Political Challenges	Cultures of the Region	Hope for the Future

Essential Question

How does unequal access to oil wealth affect the lives of Nigeria's people?

____

____

____

Who should benefit from a country's resources?

Prepare to Write

Throughout this chapter, you have explored the Essential Question in your text, journal, and On Assignment at myWorldGeography.com. Use what you've learned to write an essay on the topic of how people should handle resources in West and Central Africa. Consider the following: the resources that exist in the region, who benefits from them now, who benefited from them in the past, and the need for change in the region.

Workshop Skill: Write Body Paragraphs

Review how to outline your essay and write an introduction. Phrase the main point you want to make in your essay as a thesis statement. For example, *Nigeria does not use its resources wisely*. In your introduction, support your thesis with three facts.

In this lesson, you will learn how to write body paragraphs. Each body paragraph should develop one of the ideas you listed in the introduction that supports your thesis statement. Each body paragraph takes the idea further by giving details or evidence.

Write a Topic Sentence Start with a topic sentence. A topic sentence must clearly state the main idea of the body paragraph, connect that idea to the essay's thesis, and provide a transition from the previous paragraph. The sample body paragraph below was designed to follow the introduction paragraph.

Support the Topic Sentence With Discussion and Facts Explain your point and support it with discussion and details. Discussion sentences connect and explain your main point and supporting details. Supporting details provide the meat—the actual facts that show that what you say is true.

End With a Concluding Sentence Finish your paragraph with a sentence that reflects your topic sentence and draws together the details.

Here is a sample body paragraph:

Sample topic sentence *Nigeria does not use its resources wisely because it allows the oil industry to damage the environment.*

Supporting discussion *Although the oil industry is the country's biggest business, allowing it to harm the environment has serious consequences.*

Supporting detail *Air pollution from oil and natural gas makes the skies sooty and the air hard to breathe.*

Supporting detail *Due to pollution from oil fields, Nigerians can no longer fish in the Niger Delta.*

Supporting discussion *The loss of fish as a food source and the polluted air hurts the people living in the Niger Delta.*

Concluding sentence *To avoid these problems, Nigerians should prevent environmental damage from the oil industry.*

Write a Body Paragraph

Now write your own body paragraph for your essay.

Topic sentence

____

____

Supporting discussion

____

____

Supporting detail

____

____

Supporting detail

____

____

Supporting discussion

____

____

Concluding sentence

____

____

Draft Your Essay

Use the body paragraph above in your complete five-paragraph essay (written on another sheet of paper). Check each of your body paragraphs for a topic sentence, supporting details, and a concluding sentence.

Essential Question

Is conflict unavoidable?

Preview Before you begin this chapter, think about the Essential Question. Understanding how the Essential Question connects to your life will help you understand the chapter you are about to read.

Connect to Your Life

1 What has caused conflicts in your family, school, community, or state? Name two recent conflicts.

____

____

2 Listed in the table below are three reasons for conflicts. Rate how apt each one is to cause conflict, with 1 being likely and 5 being unlikely. To help decide, you may want to consider the conflicts you named above.

Reason for Conflict	How likely is it to cause conflict?				
Misunderstandings	1	2	3	4	5
Power struggles	1	2	3	4	5
Differences	1	2	3	4	5
Other: _________________	1	2	3	4	5

Connect to the Chapter

3 Now think about sources of conflict in a country. For example, differences in religious beliefs can lead to tension. Preview the chapter by skimming the chapter's headings, photographs, and graphics. In the web below, predict sources of conflict in Southern and Eastern Africa.

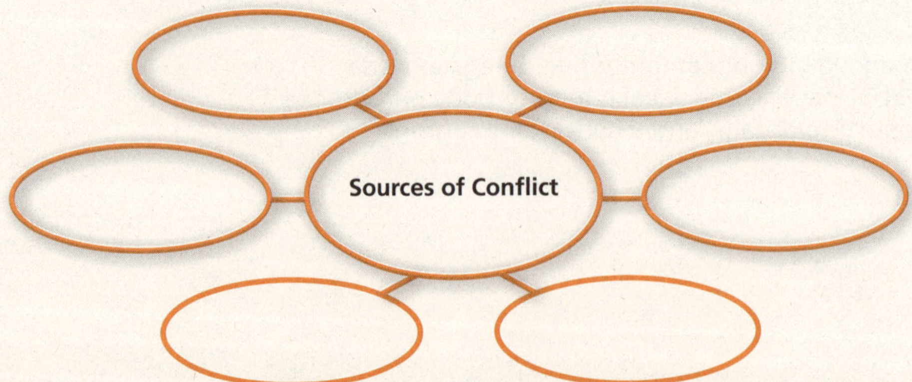

4 After reading the chapter, return to this page and use a highlighter to mark your accurate predictions.

Name _________________________ Class _________________ Date __________

Connect to myStory:
A Hopeful Song

(1) Think about ways in which your life is similar to and different from Khulekani's life. What challenges does your family face on a daily basis? How does school play a role in your life? What are your hopes for the future?

____

____

____

(2) Use this Venn diagram to compare your life with Khulekani's life. Think about family challenges, your school, and your hopes for the future.

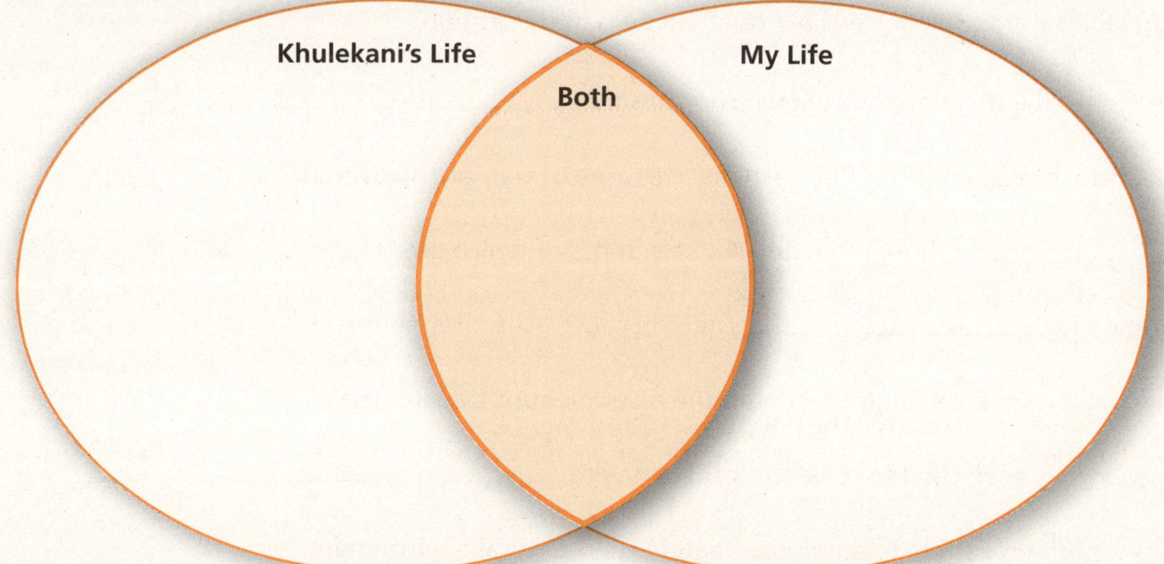

(3) On the table below, list the challenges Khulekani faces as he tries to help his family meets its goals.

Daily Life	Earning a Living	Getting an Education

(4) How do you think these challenges affect the people and nations of Southern and Eastern Africa? Write at least two ideas below.

____

Word Wise

Word Bank Choose one word from the word bank to fill in each blank. When you have finished, you will have a short summary of important ideas from the section.

Word Bank

Serengeti Plain	ecotourism
poaching	Great Rift Valley

Southern and Eastern Africa has physical features that support several different ecosystems. One unusual physical feature is the _____________________, which formed when two of Earth's plates separated, causing land to sink. The Eastern African Plateau is in this region.

Another flat area is a savanna which forms the _____________________, one of Africa's most important ecosystems. This area of flat, grass-covered plains with few trees is home to many animals, some of which are threatened by _____________________. That's because even though it is against the law, people living on or near the savanna hunt the animals. Some countries have tried to solve this problem with _____________________, which encourages visitors to admire animals in their natural environment without damaging the ecosystem.

Name _____________________ Class _____________ Date __________

Take Notes

Map Skills Use the maps in your book to make a key and to label the Places to Know on the outline map below.

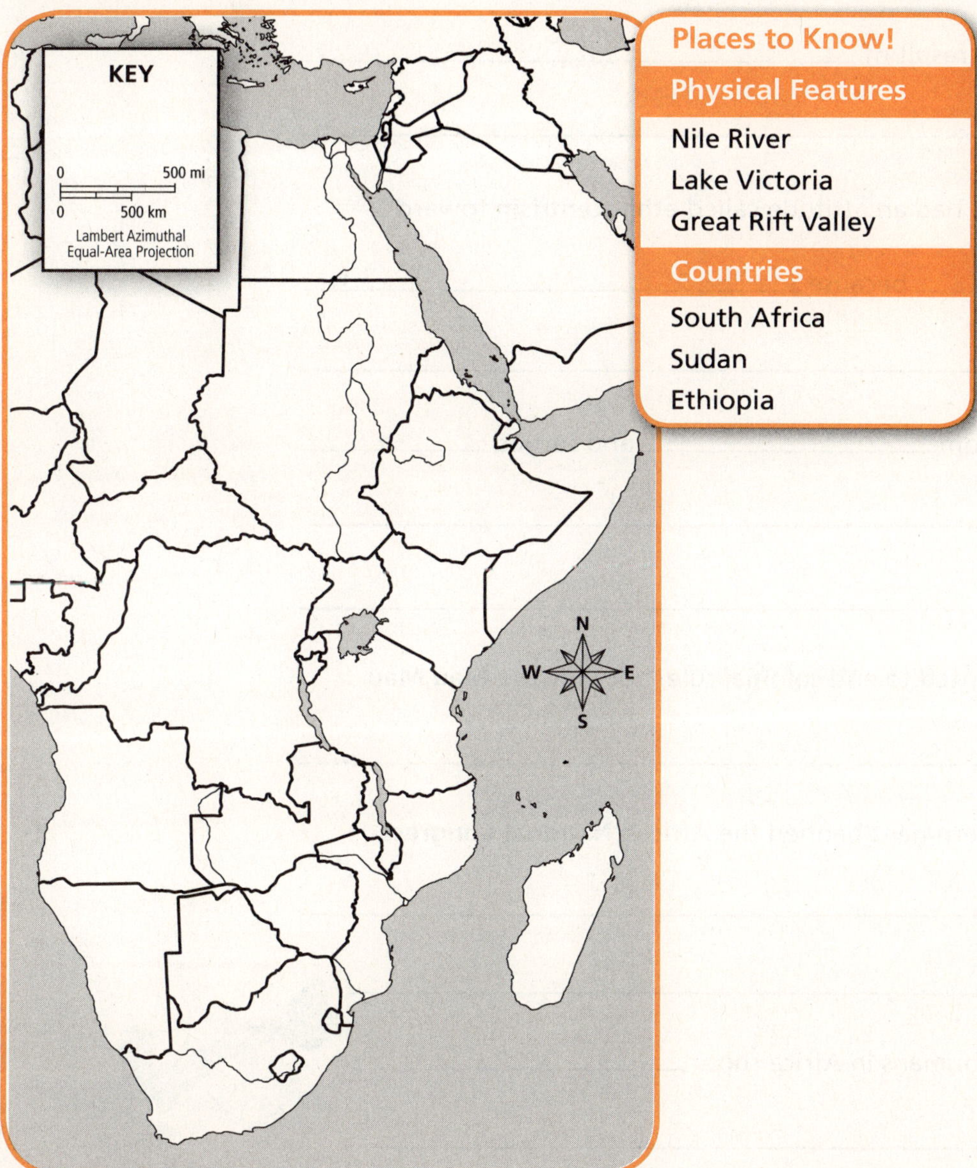

Places to Know!

Physical Features

Nile River

Lake Victoria

Great Rift Valley

Countries

South Africa

Sudan

Ethiopia

Essential Question

How do you think the lack of resources in some countries might cause conflict? How might the abundance of resources in other countries cause conflict?

____

____

____

Word Wise

Sentence Builder Complete the sentences using the information you learned in this section. Include terminal punctuation.

1. **Apartheid** was the result of _______________________________

____

2. European colonists had an attitude called **ethnocentrism** toward

________________________ because _________________________________

____

3. The **Boers** came from _______________________ and settled _______________

____

____

4. Many Kenyans wanted to end colonial rule, but only the **Mau Mau**

____

5. South Africa's government banned the **African National Congress**

because ____

____

6. **Fossils** of ancient humans in Africa show _______________________

____

THE RHODES COLOSSUS

Name _________________________ Class _____________________ Date ___________

Take Notes

Sequence Use what you have read about the history of Southern and Eastern Africa to complete the timeline below. For each date given, write the event.

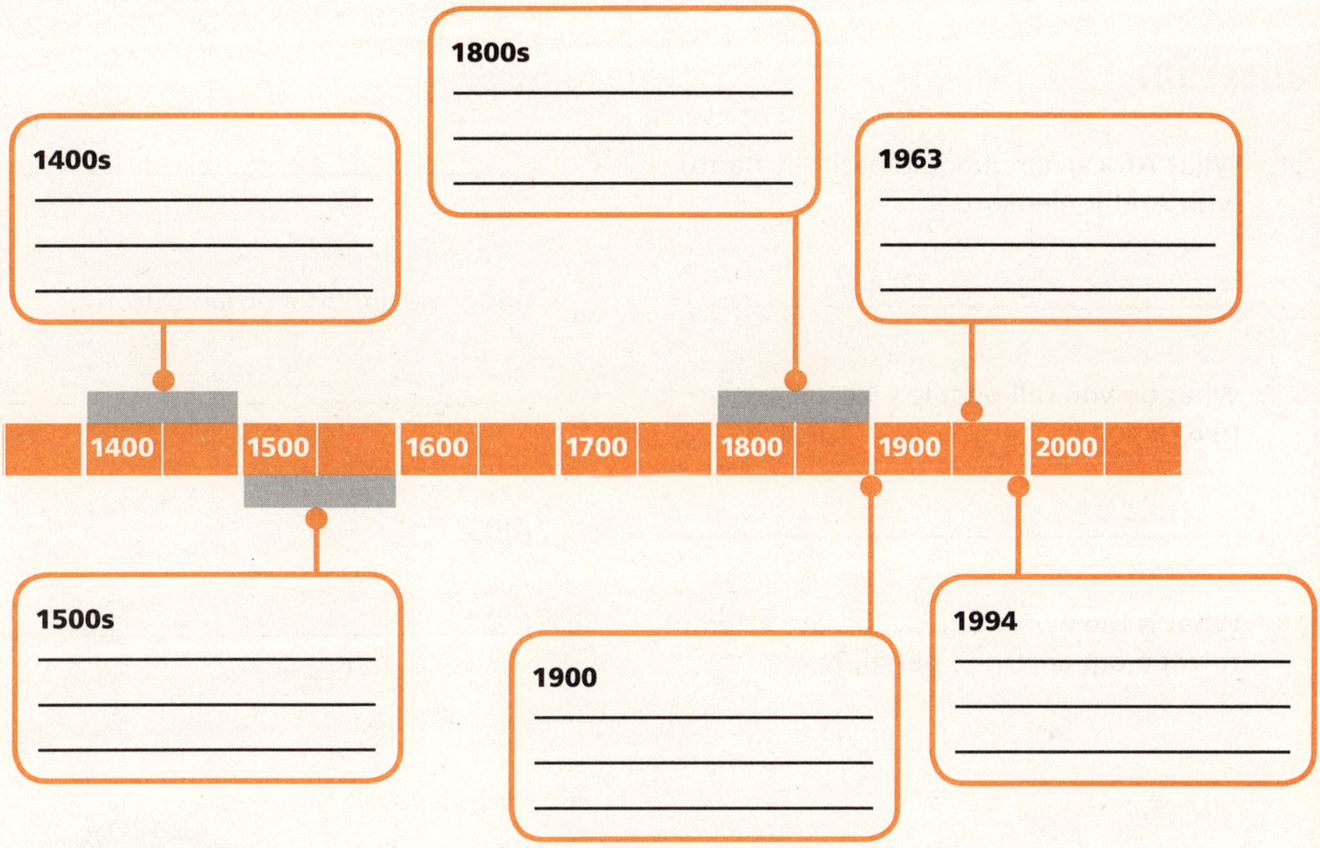

Apartheid in South Africa ended without civil war or large-scale ethnic conflict. What do you think made this possible?

____

____

____

Word Wise

Vocabulary Quiz Show Some quiz shows ask a question and expect the contestant to give the answer. In other shows, the contestant is given an answer and must supply the question. If the blank is in the question column, write the question that would result in the answer given. If the question is supplied, write the appropriate answer.

QUESTION

1. What African language is basically Bantu with Arabic elements?

2. _________________________________

3. What do you call people who are native to a region?

4. _________________________________

5. What is the word for a deliberate attempt to wipe out an entire people?

ANSWER

1. _________________________________

2. nongovernmental organization

3. _________________________________

4. AIDS

5. _________________________________

Name _______________________________ Class _____________________________ Date ____________

Take Notes

Compare and Contrast Use what you read about life in Southern and
Eastern Africa today to complete the table below. For each factor listed, give
a contrasting example from the section. If the contrast between the two has
led to a conflict, circle yes in the last column. Otherwise, circle no. The first
row is completed for you.

Factor	Contrasting Examples		Has it Caused Conflict?
language	Swahili as a common language	English in former British colonies	Yes (No)
ethnicity		Africans in southern Sudan	Yes No
political system	single-party rule in Zimbabwe		Yes No

Look at the row(s) in which you circled yes. Write an explanation of why
these contrasts caused conflict.

____

____

____

____

? Essential Question

**In the countries of Sudan, Rwanda, Kenya, and South Africa, what
has caused ethnic violence?**

____

____

____

____

Prepare to Write

Throughout this chapter, you have explored the Essential Question in your text, journal, and On Assignment at myWorldGeography.com. Use what you learned to write an essay about why the nations in Southern and Eastern Africa should teach their citizens to avoid conflict. Consider the following factors: ethnic, religious, and political differences that exist in the region, the economic challenges these countries face, the ways conflict has shaped African history, and the benefits of avoiding future conflicts.

Workshop Skill: Write a Conclusion

Review how to outline your essay, write an introduction, and develop body paragraphs. Consider the main point you want to make in your essay and phrase it as a thesis statement—for example: *Teaching people to avoid conflict will improve the future for Southern and Eastern Africa.* In your introduction, list three ideas that support this thesis. In your body paragraphs, develop one idea in each paragraph, using details and evidence to support it. For example, you might write *Conflict has interfered with Southern and Eastern Africa's ability to meet its economic challenges.* Follow this by giving specific examples of why the statement is true.

In this lesson, you will learn how to summarize your arguments in a conclusion. The conclusion of an essay has three goals: It must restate your thesis and tell readers why it matters to them. It must briefly acknowledge challenges to your argument and remind readers why your argument makes sense. Finally, it must tell readers what you want them to think or do.

Connect With a Restatement Start with a sentence that recalls your topic and thesis. Emphasize the importance of your argument by telling readers how the issue affects people outside the region. Remember to shape that sentence in a way that moves smoothly from the final body paragraph.

Answer Challenges With a Rebuttal Next, imagine you are debating your issue face to face. What arguments would someone give against your thesis? In one or two sentences, identify one of these arguments and explain why it is incorrect or not convincing. For example, you might note that it will cost money to teach new attitudes but that the poverty caused by conflict will actually cost more.

Call to Action Finish your conclusion with a specific request for action by answering the question: What can readers do to help solve the problem? Discuss ways that people can change their thinking. You may also describe some actions people can take.

Sample Conclusion

This conclusion demonstrates all three parts:

Restatement *For all these reasons, people around the world should support the goal of teaching Africans to avoid conflict. When African countries prosper, they will demand less international aid and contribute more to the global economy.*

Rebuttal *Of course teaching conflict avoidance will cost the rest of us money, but cleaning up the problems caused by African conflict will cost us much more in the long run.*

Call to Action *The nations of the world must think in terms of investing in a shared future and building a roof to shelter all of us. Write your Congressional representative today to promote funding for conflict-resolution programs in Africa.*

Draft Your Conclusion

Now write each part of the conclusion for your essay:

Restatement _______________________________________

____

____

____

Rebuttal _______________________________________

____

____

____

Call to Action _______________________________________

____

____

____

Draft Your Essay

Make sure your conclusion restates your thesis, includes a response to anticipated challenges, and has a clearly stated call to action. Use your conclusion at the end of your five-paragraph essay. Write the essay on another piece of paper.

How much does geography shape a country?

Preview Before you begin this chapter, think about the Essential Question. Understanding how the Essential Question connects to your life will help you understand the chapter you are about to read.

Connect to Your Life

1. Think about how the geographic elements in the table below have affected your life. Complete the table below with your ideas.

Personal Influence of Geographic Elements				
Parks, Lakes, Rivers	Local Weather	Local Crops	Size of School	Recreational Activities

2. In what ways can these elements affect each other? For example, in what way can cold weather affect the type of recreational activities in a region?

____

____

Connect to the Chapter

3. Before you read the chapter, flip through every page and note the red headings, maps, and other pictures. Predict ways in which geography has influenced families and communities in North Africa. List your ideas in the table below.

Influences of Geographic Elements on a Country				
Physical Features	Climate	Natural Resources	Population	Culture

4. After reading the chapter, return to this page. Were your predictions accurate? Why or why not?

____

____

Name _________________________________ Class _______________________________ Date _____________

Connect to myStory: Shaimaa's Neighborhood

(1) What challenges face your family every day? How does school play a role in your life? What are your hopes for the future?

____

____

(2) Use this Venn diagram to compare your life with Shaimaa's life. Think about family challenges, school, and hopes for the future.

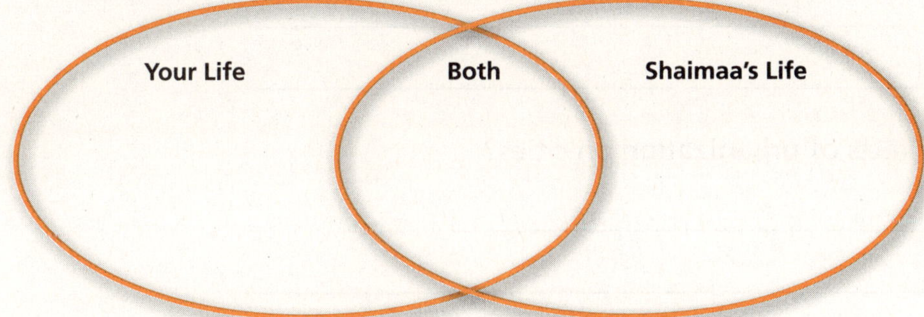

(3) In this graphic organizer, list the challenges Shaimaa faces as she tries to help her family to meet its goals.

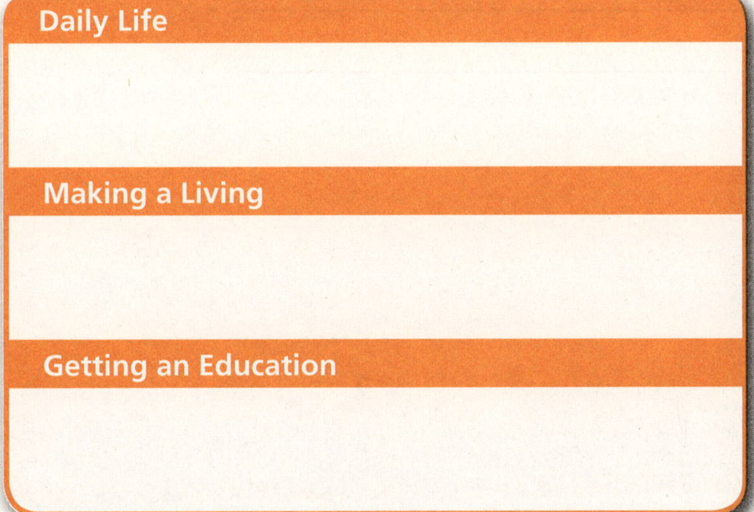

(4) How do you think these challenges are affecting people in North Africa? Write your predictions.

____

____

Word Wise

Words In Context For each question below, write an answer that shows your understanding of the boldfaced key term.

1. Why do people of the Sahara live near **oases**?

   ____

   ____

2. How does a river change at its **delta**? How does a river's **delta** change the surrounding land?

   ____

   ____

3. What are some effects of **urbanization** on cities?

   ____

   ____

4. Why do **nomads** in the Sahara Desert live by herding animals instead of by farming?

   ____

   ____

Name _____________________________   Class _____________________   Date __________

Take Notes

Map Skills Use the maps in your book to make a key and to label the Places to Know on the outline map below.

Places to Know!

Physical Features	Countries
Sahara Desert	Egypt
Atlas Mountains	Morocco
Nile River	Algeria
Suez Canal	

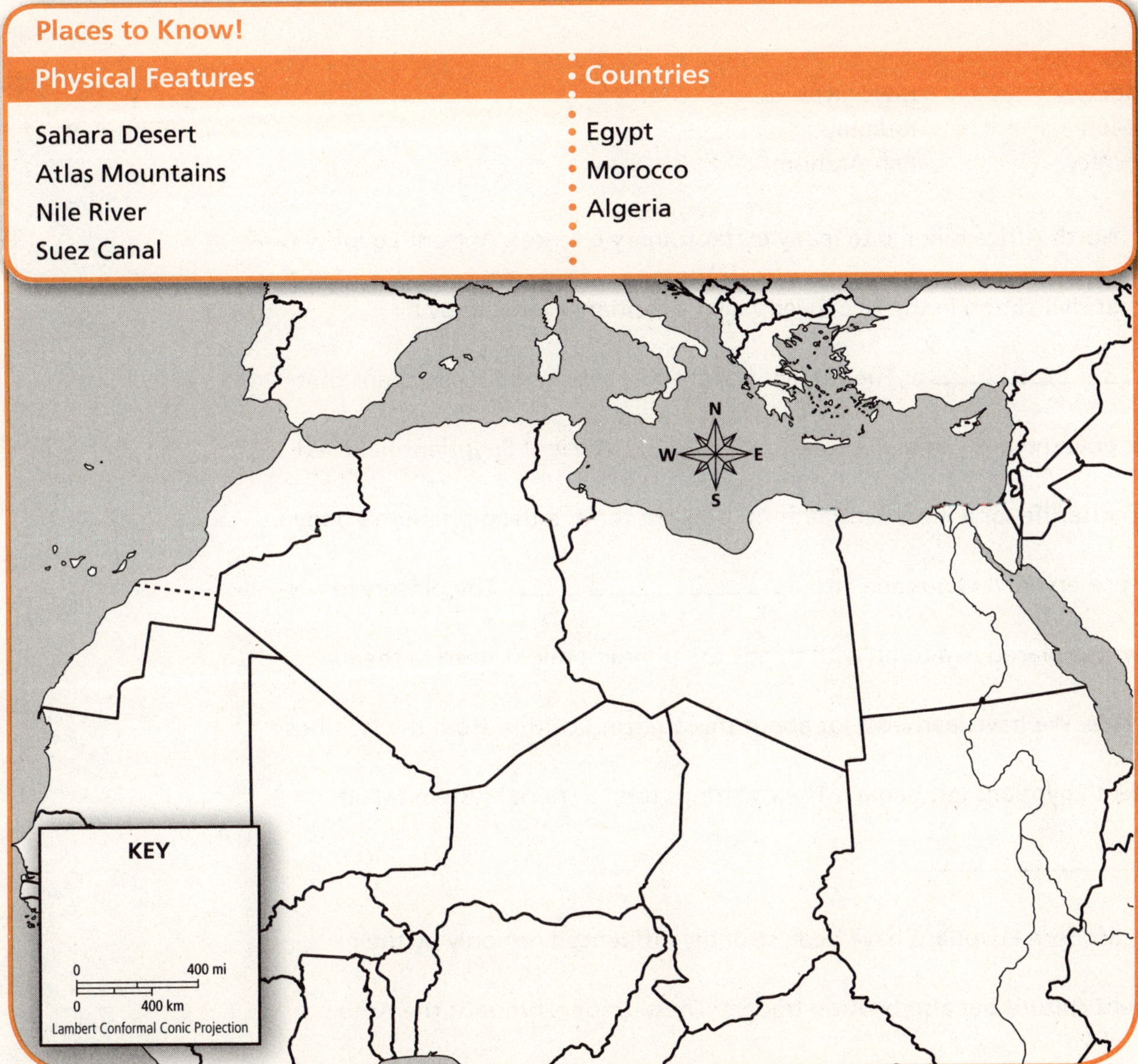

Essential Question

How does water shape human settlement patterns in North Africa?

____

____

____

Word Wise

Word Bank Choose one word from the word bank to fill in each blank. When you have finished, you will have a short summary of important ideas from the section.

Word Bank

Berbers	hieroglyphics
pharaoh	mummy
theocracy	Pan-Arabism

North Africa is home to many extraordinary cultures. Ancient Egypt was a great civilization in the Nile River Valley. Egyptians were led by a ____________________. The citizens believed he was a god. This means that their government was a ____________________. Ancient Egyptians believed in an afterlife, or a life after death. To prepare for it, a dead pharaoh's body was preserved. It was made into a ____________________. The preserved body was placed in a tomb with things the pharaoh might need in the afterlife. We have learned a lot about this amazing culture from the writings ancient Egyptians left behind. Their writings used a special system called ____________________.

Modern Egyptians have been strongly influenced not only by their ancient culture but also by Arab traders. These traders brought the Arabic language to Egyptians and their neighbors in western North Africa, the ____________________. Today some people in the region support ____________________, or the idea that this common language should unite nations.

Name ___________________________ Class ___________________ Date ___________

Take Notes

Cause and Effect Use what you have read about the history of North Africa to complete the table below. Under each column, list effects of each culture on the history of North Africa.

Impact of Cultures on North Africa		
Ancient Egypt	**Arab North Africa**	**European Rule**

Essential Question

How did physical geography shape the development of ancient Egypt?

____

____

____

Name _______________________ Class _______________________ Date ___________

Word Wise

Sentence Builder Complete the sentences using the information you learned in this section. Include terminal punctuation.

1. A nation's **gross domestic product** tells _______________________

____

2. The **Copts**, who belong to a minority group in Egypt, are the largest

_______________________ in the Middle East, yet they are _______________________

____

3. The **human development index** includes quality of life factors such as

____

4. The **gross domestic product per capita** is a measure of _______________________

____

5. Egyptians who belong to the **Muslim Brotherhood** _______________________

____

6. Those who believe in **secularism** _______________________

____

Name ______________________________ Class ____________________ Date ____________

Take Notes

Main Idea and Details Use what you read about the current governments and political issues in North Africa to complete this concept web. In each labeled oval, list details about that country's government and the political issues the country faces.

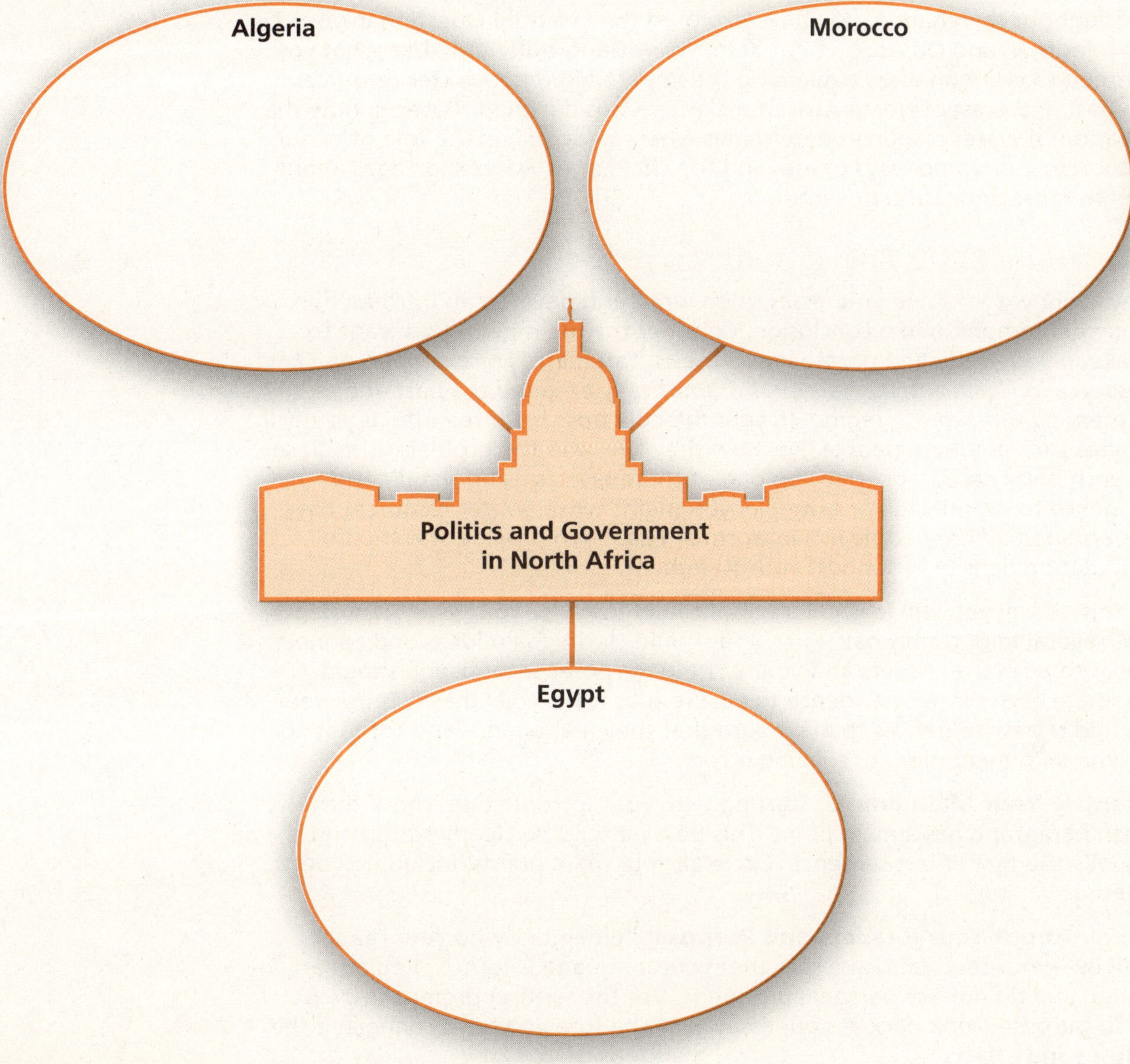

Essential Question

How has oil affected life in North Africa today?

____

____

____

How much does geography shape a country?

Prepare to Write

Throughout this chapter, you have explored the Essential Question in your text, journal, and On Assignment at myWorldGeography.com. Use what you learned to write an essay explaining the impact of limited water resources on past and present North African societies. Consider the following: how the location of water resources determines where people live; the role of water resources in shaping ways of life; and the challenges water shortages might create for societies and governments.

Workshop Skill: Revise Your Essay

Review how to outline your essay, then write and develop an introduction, body paragraphs, and a conclusion. Consider the main point you want to make in your essay and phrase it as a thesis statement. For example: *As a key resource in North Africa, water has dramatically affected the past and present cultures of the region.* In your introduction, list three effects you will discuss such as where people live, how they live, and the problems they face. In each body paragraph, develop one of these effects using details and evidence to support it. For example, you might write, *Water resources have determined where people live in North Africa.* Then provide statistics for population density to support your statement.

In this lesson, you will learn more about how to revise your essay. Revision has several important goals: First, you should clarify main ideas and connect them to both the readers and your writing purpose. Second, you should evaluate each piece of evidence to ensure that it fits your thesis. Third, you should review sentences to make sure that they make sense and contain no grammar, punctuation, or spelling errors.

Identify Your Main Points Starting with your introduction, check that each paragraph has a main point. This point should be clearly stated and is usually the first or last sentence. Circle all your main points, including your thesis.

Think About Your Readers and Purpose Remember who your reader will be—your teacher. Make sure that your language is formal. Replace any slang, and do not use personal pronouns. Use the writing prompt to guide your purpose. Look back at your essay to make sure you have connected the causes and effects.

Evaluate Your Evidence Reread each circled main point. Then carefully read the rest of the paragraph. Does the evidence support the main point? Is the evidence organized in a logical manner? For instance, you might want to list examples from history in chronological order. Also make sure the evidence supports your thesis. You may need to reword your thesis slightly to fit the points you've made. Sentences that don't support the thesis and main ideas should be eliminated.

Be Clear and Correct Now read your essay aloud. Never skip this step! Hearing your sentences will help you notice when they don't flow or if they don't make sense. Ask yourself what you meant to say and use that restatement to rewrite confusing sentences. Then reread silently or use a computer grammar and spelling checker to find and correct any errors.

Here is a sample edited paragraph. The notes in parentheses explain the major revisions:

The location of water in North Africa has long influenced where people live. For example, ancient Egyptians built their civilization in the Nile River Valley, which gave them access to the river's water for many uses. Yearly floods made the soil rich for agriculture, and the river offered transportation. ~~Work on the river also helped to shape a strong central~~
(not related to the main point)
~~government.~~ About half of today's North Africans still live in Egypt, and
(informal)
almost all of them live near the Nile River. ~~That's~~ They want to be where the water is. Many other North Africans live along the coast of the Mediterranean Sea. Nomads travel the deserts and stop at oases to access water. Each of these population centers have grown due to the need for
(clarifies cause and effect relationship)
water.

Revise Your Essay

Now look critically at one paragraph from your essay and make revisions to improve it. Write your corrected paragraph below.

____

____

____

____

____

Draft Your Essay

Copy the revised paragraph into your essay. Use it as a guide in revising the remaining paragraphs. Make sure to check each paragraph for a main idea, supporting evidence, and appropriate spelling, grammar, and punctuation.

Name _______________________________ Class _______________________________ Date ____________

How much does geography shape a country?

Preview Before you begin this chapter, think about the Essential Question. Understanding how the Essential Question connects to your life will help you understand the chapter you are about to read.

Connect to Your Life

(1) What are some ways in which geography shapes your life? Think about how you are influenced by climate, geographic events, or a shortage of resources in your community. Also consider location issues such as urban density or geographic isolation, or economic impacts such as tourism to geographic points of interest. Fill in the table with your responses.

Personal Influence of Geographic Elements				
Parks, Lakes, Rivers	• Local Weather	• Local Crops	• Size of School	• Recreational Activities

(2) How would your family's life change if you lived in a different location?

____

____

Connect to the Chapter

(3) Before you read the chapter, flip through every page and note the headings, maps, and pictures. Think about ways that geography's impact on families and communities applies to nations as well. List your ideas in the table below.

Influences of Geographic Elements on a Country				
Physical Features	• Climate	• Natural Resources	• Population	• Culture

(4) After you read the chapter, return to this page. Which of your predictions was inaccurate? Explain why they were wrong.

____

____

Connect to myStory: Hanan's Call to Care

1. Think about ways in which your life is like Hanan's life. What are your cultural beliefs? Have you ever wanted to do something that is unusual in your family or community? Explain.

____

____

____

2. Use this Venn diagram to compare your life with Hanan's life. Think about daily life, plans for the future, and expectations of family and community.

3. List the challenges that Hanan faces as she tries to plan her future in the table below.

Cultural Rules	Geographic Limits	Political Situations

4. How do you think these challenges affect the citizens in the nations of Arabia and Iraq?

____

____

____

Word Wise

Vocabulary Quiz Show Some quiz shows ask a question and expect the contestant to give the answer. In other shows, the contestant is given an answer and must supply the question. If the blank is in the question column, write the question that would result in the answer given. If the question is supplied, write the appropriate answer.

QUESTION	ANSWER
(1) ________________________________	(1) desalinization
(2) What do you call the large pieces of Earth's crust?	(2) ________________________________
(3) ________________________________	(3) fossil fuel
(4) What word describes a nation in which most of the population lives in cities?	(4) ________________________________
(5) ________________________________	(5) majority

Name ______________________________ Class __________________ Date __________

Take Notes

Map Skills Use the maps in your book to make a key and to label the Places to Know on the outline map below.

Places to Know!

Physical Features	Countries	Cities
Tigris River	Iraq	Baghdad
Euphrates River	United Arab Emirates	Riyadh
Syrian Desert	Yemen	Mecca
Rub'al Khali		
Persian Gulf		
Red Sea		

Essential Question

What features of Arabia and Iraq depend on the region's geography? What features do not depend on its geography?

____

____

____

Word Wise

Crossword Puzzle The clues describe key terms from this section. Fill in the numbered *Across* boxes with the correct key terms. Then, do the same with the *Down* clues.

Across	Down
1. a Muslim house of worship	4. worshipping only one god
2. a culture that has writing and where people do many different types of jobs	5. the holy book of Islam
3. a group with less than half of the population	6. an all-powerful leader who has complete control over a nation
	7. an Islamic political and religious leader

Name _____________________________ Class _____________________________ Date _____________

Take Notes

Summarize Use what you have read about the history of Arabia and Iraq to complete the table below. In each column, list the main ideas about the topic.

Early Civilizations	Birth of Islam	Muslim Culture	Modern Life

Essential Question

How has geography shaped the history of Arabia and Iraq? Are there parts of its history that did not depend on its geography?

____

____

____

Name _________________________________ Class _____________________________ Date ___________

Word Wise

Words In Context For each question below, write an answer that shows your understanding of the boldfaced key term.

(1) Why do most Muslims in Arabia and Iraq reject **terrorism**?

____

____

(2) What is **fundamentalism**?

____

____

(3) Why does economic growth depend partly on **entrepreneurship**?

____

____

(4) Why do women wear **hijab** in some parts of the Arab world?

____

____

(5) How has the concept of **jihad** caused problems for Westerners in the Arab world?

____

____

(6) What effect does **Islamism** have on politics and society?

____

____

Name _________________________________ Class _____________________ Date ___________

Take Notes

Cause and Effect Use what you read about life in Arabia and Iraq today to complete the table below. In the left column, list at least three factors that have strong influences on life in the region. In the right column, fill in the effect of those influences.

Influences	Effects

Essential Question

What are some challenges the region's nations could face if oil and gas reserves run out?

____

____

____

Essential Question Writer's Workshop

How much does geography shape a country?

Prepare to Write

Throughout this chapter, you have explored the Essential Question in your text, journal, and On Assignment at myWorldGeography.com. Use what you've learned about Arabia and Iraq to write a persuasive essay in response to this question: Do Arabia's and Iraq's past and present circumstances result mainly from geography or from other factors?

Workshop Skill: Understand the Four Types of Essays

One of the most challenging types of essays to write is the persuasive essay because it expresses an opinion and strives to get readers to agree. The opinion is the essay's "thesis," and it must be stated in the introduction. Remember there is no incorrect opinion; what is important is to thoroughly support your view position.

Write a Thesis Statement First, decide your answer to the question posed. Do you think that the region's past and present circumstances result mainly from geography or from other factors? If you think it was other factors, identify them. Then write a complete sentence expressing your idea. Include the key words from the question in your answer. Here's an example:

Culture, more than geography, has determined the past and present circumstances in Arabia and Iraq.

Your thesis statement ____

____

Write an Introduction Your thesis must reflect the essay's main arguments. Think of a logical way to organize three important arguments that support your opinion. In this case, time is a good way to organize ideas. Notice how this mini-outline states arguments in historical sequence. Each also shows a cause-and-effect relationship that answers the prompt question.

Reason One Early civilizations in the region created the model for later cultures.

Reason Two The religion of Islam became both the main cultural influence and the main cause of dissent in the region.

Reason Three Conflicts between traditional and modern cultures led to current ways of life and conflicts.

Organize Your Essay

Like all essays, the persuasive essay will have an introduction, three body paragraphs, and a conclusion. Organize your essay following the model shown here.

Paragraph 1: Introduction Remember to open with a catchy question or statement, known as a "hook" to get readers interested. Expand your thesis statement to suggest the three arguments you listed.

Paragraph 2: First Body Paragraph State your first argument and use at least two details to support it.

Topic sentence *Early civilizations in the region created models for later cultures.*
Detail 1 *Assyria became the model for a later Persian empire.*

Detail 2 ____

Concluding Sentence *These early influences remained important as time went on.*

Paragraph 3: Second Body Paragraph Explain your second argument. In the example, notice how time order transition words help the reader move into this new paragraph.

Topic Sentence *In the 600s, the new religion of Islam began to shape*

____

Detail 1 ____

Detail 2 ____

Concluding Sentence _______________________________________

Paragraph 4: Third Body Paragraph Explan your third argument. Add detail to the topic sentence given below and use a time order transition to move from the previous paragraph.

Topic Sentence *Even today,* ________________________________

Detail 1 ____

Detail 2 ____

Concluding Sentence _______________________________________

Paragraph 5: Conclusion In the conclusion, summarize the main arguments that support your thesis. End by relating your opinion to a current event or a probable future event.

____

To interact successfully with the people in the Arabian region, people

around the world must _______________________________________

Draft Your Essay

Write your essay on another sheet of paper. When you're done, proofread it with a partner.

Essential Question

Is conflict unavoidable?

Preview Before you begin this chapter, think about the Essential Question. Understanding how the Essential Question connects to your life will help you understand the chapter you are about to read.

Connect to Your Life

① What has caused conflicts in your family, school, community, or state? Name two recent conflicts.

____

② Listed in the table below are three reasons that conflicts begin. Rate how likely each one is to cause conflict, with 1 being likely and 5 being unlikely. To help decide, you may want to consider the conflicts you named.

Reason for Conflict	How likely is it to cause conflict?				
Misunderstandings	1	2	3	4	5
Power struggles	1	2	3	4	5
Differences	1	2	3	4	5
Other: ________________	1	2	3	4	5

Connect to the Chapter

③ Preview the chapter by skimming the headings, photographs, and graphics. Predict sources of conflict in the region in the web below. Color-code the conflicts as avoidable or unavoidable. For example, red might be avoidable and green unavoidable.

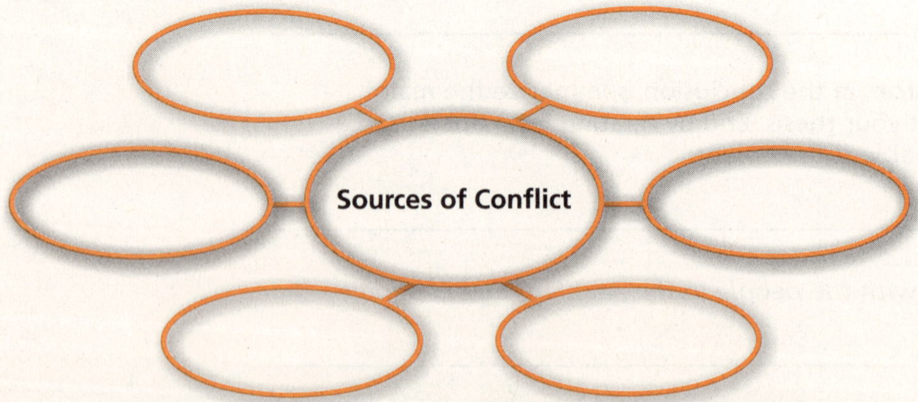

④ After reading the chapter, circle your predictions that were correct.

Name _________________________ Class _________________________ Date __________

Connect to myStory: Maayan and Muhammad

① Think about a person or group of people who live in this country but who are unfamiliar to you. Are you afraid of these people? Do they make you feel uneasy? Is it because you do not know very much about them?

____

____

____

② Maayan and Muhammad live in the same nation yet feel apart from each other. Fill in the Venn diagram below to compare Maayan's life with Muhammad's. Think about their families, schools, and concerns.

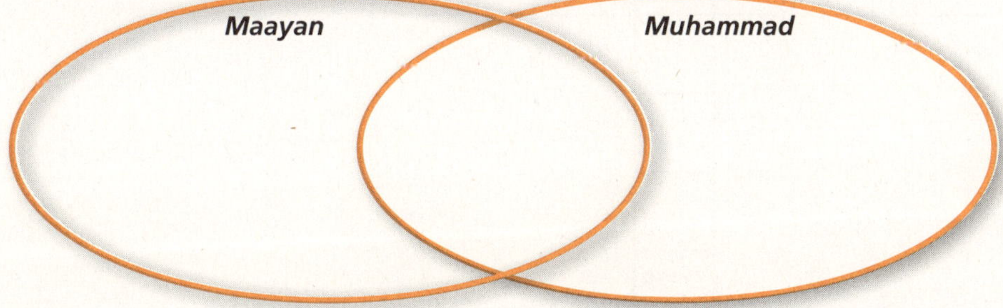

③ Think about the concerns Maayan and Muhammad mention in their lives. What does this tell you about life in Israel today?

____

____

____

Word Wise

Crossword Puzzle The clues describe key terms from this section. Fill in the numbered *Across* with the correct key terms. Then, do the same with the *Down* clues.

Across	Down
1. wells tap into these underground water sources	4. crops thrive in this area that stretches from the Mediterranean coast to the Persian Gulf
2. a member of a religion that combines others teachings with Islam	5. a kind of Islam similar to Shia Islam
3. the dry area on the opposite side of the mountains where the precipitation falls	

Name _________________________________ Class ___________________________ Date ______________

Take Notes

Map Skills Use the maps in your book to make a key and to label the Places to Know on the outline map below.

Places to Know!

Physical Features	Territories	Countries	City
Lebanon Mountains	Gaza Strip	Israel	Jerusalem
Syrian Desert	West Bank	Lebanon	
Euphrates River		Syria	
Jordan River		Jordan	
Mediterranean Sea			

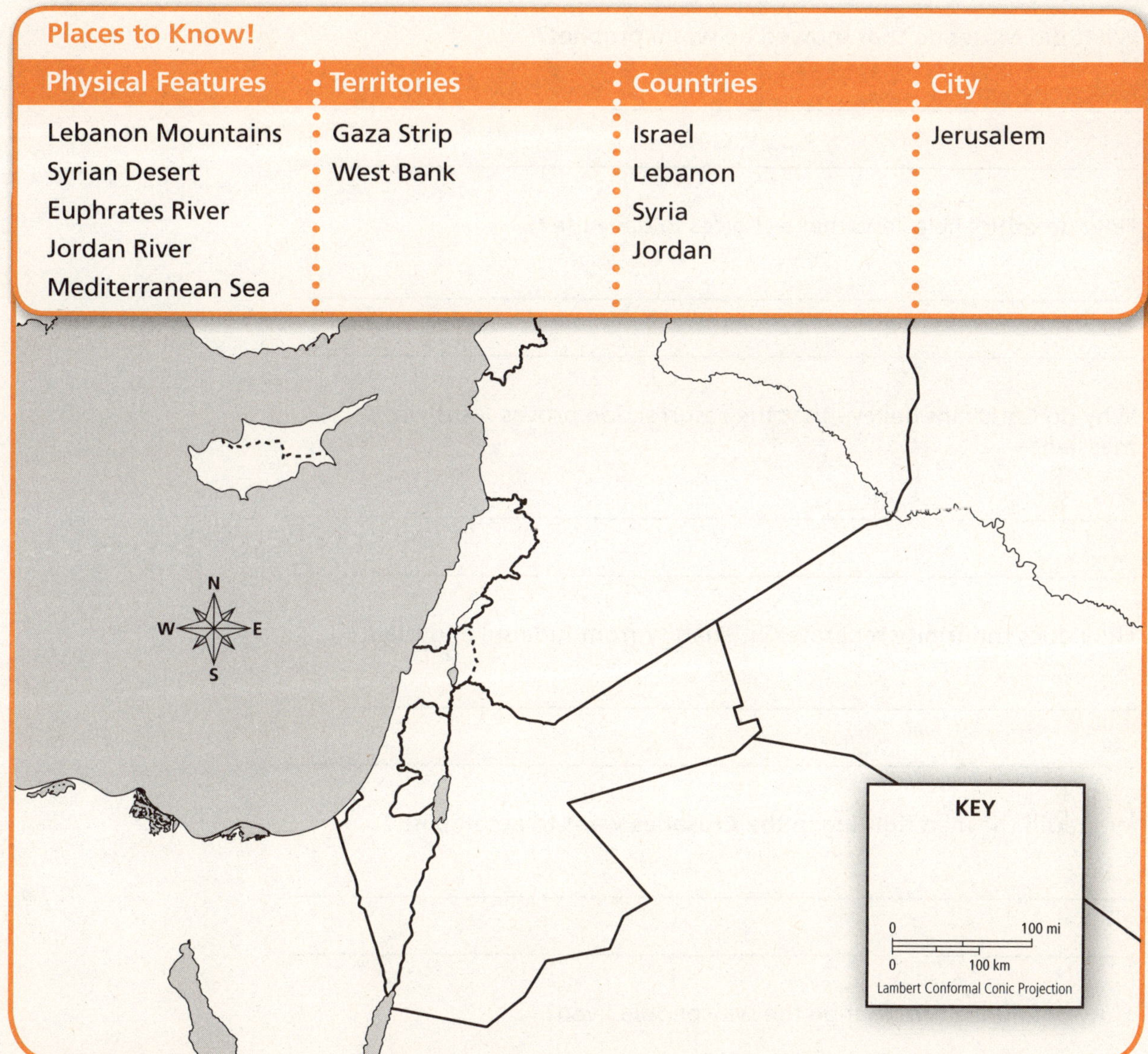

Essential Question

Describe steps that Israel and its neighbors have taken to reduce conflict over water resources.

____

____

____

Word Wise

Words In Context For each question below, write an answer that shows your understanding of the boldfaced key term.

1. What did Moses do that showed he was a **prophet**?

   ____

   ____

2. How do **ethics** help Jews make choices in daily life?

   ____

   ____

3. Why do Christians believe that the resurrection proves Jesus was a **messiah**?

   ____

   ____

4. How does the **Trinity** separate Christianity from Judaism and Islam?

   ____

   ____

5. What did the men fighting in the **Crusades** want to accomplish?

   ____

   ____

6. How did **agriculture** change the way people lived?

   ____

   ____

7. What were the goals of **Zionism**?

   ____

   ____

8. Why did **anti-Semitism** lead millions of Jews to leave Europe?

   ____

Name ________________________________ Class ____________________ Date ____________

Take Notes

Compare and Contrast Use what you have read about the history of Israel and its neighbors to complete the table with important events and beliefs from each era.

Jewish Era	Christian Era	Muslim Era	Modern Era
Events:	**Events:**	**Events:**	**Events:**
Beliefs:	**Beliefs:**	**Beliefs:**	**Beliefs:**

Essential Question

Give an example of a conflict in the region. Could it be avoided? If so, explain how.

____

____

____

Word Wise

Vocabulary Quiz Show Some quiz shows ask a question and expect the contestant to give the answer. In other shows, the contestant is given an answer and must supply the question. If the blank is in the question column, write the question that would result in the answer given. If the question is supplied, write the appropriate answer.

QUESTION

ANSWER

1. What do you call the areas where Israelis built homes in the Palestinian Territories during the 1970s and 1980s?

1. _______________________

2. _______________________

2. capital

3. What is the type of government in which an elected parliament selects the prime minister?

3. _______________________

4. _______________________

4. autocracy

5. What is the name for a government in which a powerful king passes leadership to his son?

5. _______________________

6. _______________________

6. Intifada

Name _______________________________ Class _____________________________ Date ____________

Take Notes

Summarize Use what you have read about Israel and its neighbors to complete the table below. For each topic give details and then write a one-sentence summary. At the bottom, write a three-sentence overall summary about the region.

Region's Different Political Systems	**Standard of Living**
Details:	Details:
Summary:	Summary:
Palestinian-Israeli Conflict	**Region's Global Importance**
Details:	Details:
Summary:	Summary:

Overall Summary:

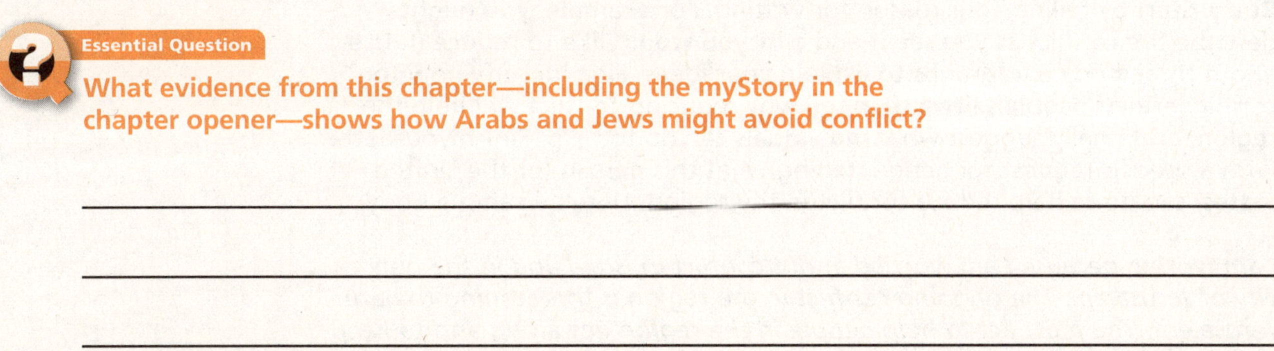

Essential Question

What evidence from this chapter—including the myStory in the chapter opener—shows how Arabs and Jews might avoid conflict?

____

____

____

Name ________________________________ Class ____________________________ Date ____________

Essential Question Writer's Workshop

Is conflict unavoidable?

Prepare to Write

Throughout this chapter, you have explored the Essential Question in your text, journal, and On Assignment at myWorldGeography.com. Now you will write a formal letter to answer the question, "How can conflict be reduced or eliminated in this region?"

Workshop Skill: Write a Letter

First, decide who will receive your letter. You might write a letter to the editor of your local paper, to a politician or official of the United States government, or to a government official in a nation in the area (Israel or one of its neighbors). Your letter will tell the recipient ways in which you think he or she can reduce conflict in the region.

Who will receive your letter? ______________________________________

Date, Heading, and Greeting In a formal letter, the heading includes your return address and the date in the upper right corner, and the full name and address of the recipient on the left. Skip a line and write the greeting. Most letters use "Dear" and the recipient's name. Use a title such as *Dr., Mrs.,* or *Senator* followed by the person's last name and a colon. Here is an example:

7 Ingram Hill Road
Canton, KY 42211 U.S.A.
May 24, 2012

Mayor Nir Barkat
Jerusalem Town Hall
1234 Jerusalem Avenue
Jerusalem, Israel

Dear Mayor Barkat:

Body Start by telling your reason for writing. For example, you might describe the conflict as you see it and why you would like to reduce it. Use about three body paragraphs to explain your ideas. First identify how the conflict affects people's lives, then tell why reducing conflict will help the region, and finally suggest what individuals can do to help. Finish your letter with a specific request for action, telling what this person (or the United States) can do to help reduce conflict in the region. Here's a sample body:

I am writing because I am worried about conflict in Israel and in the holy city of Jerusalem. The ongoing conflict in the region is threatening to harm Jerusalem. You must act to help people in the region get along and to keep this special city safe.

Since Jerusalem is important to people of many different religions, I think you should try to build a bridge between religions. You can do this with your personal example. Visit some churches or mosques in Jerusalem. Show that you respect these other faiths and their attachment to the city. You could even start an organization that brings Jewish, Christian, and Muslim religious leaders together. You could also invite some leaders of these communities to be part of the city's government. It would be helpful to get ideas from everyone.

Conclusion, Closing, and Signature Conclude by briefly restating your main point. If you want the recipient to take action, such as working to pass a law or printing your letter in the newspaper, state that. Then skip a line and write a closing such as "Yours truly" followed by a comma. Sign your full name.

Draft Your Letter

Use the format below to write the first draft of your letter.

(your address and date; do not put your name) ______________________

____

____

______________________ **(name and address of recipient)**

____

____

____

Dear ______________________

Body ______________________

____

Conclusion ______________________

____

Closing ______________________

Your signature ______________________

Finalize Your Letter

Congratulations! You have drafted a formal letter. Remember to follow the steps of the writing process to revise and edit it. Proofread carefully to ensure all the spelling, punctuation, and grammar are correct. Then neatly copy the letter onto a clean sheet of paper.

Essential Question

What are the challenges of diversity?

Preview Before you begin this chapter, think about the Essential Question. Understanding how the Essential Question connects to your life will help you understand the chapter you are about to read.

Connect to Your Life

(1) Think about a time when you learned about a new culture. Name two ways in which the culture differed from your own.

____

____

(2) Think about how there is a wide range of differences in the likes and dislikes of a group of people. Think about some general ways in which people express their differences in taste. Fill in the table below with your ideas.

Categories	Clothing	Food	Music	Interests
Expressions of Different Taste				

Connect to the Chapter

(3) Preview the chapter by skimming the chapter's headings, photographs, and graphics. In the table below, predict the kind of challenges that diversity might present to the people of Iran, Turkey, and Cyprus. An example is given in the ethnic category. Fill in a prediction of your own in each of the other columns.

Types of Diversity	Ethnic	Religious	Political	Linguistic
Challenges	People from different ethnic groups may have different traditions and gender roles.			

(4) After you read the chapter, return to your predictions above. Did anything you learned about diversity in Iran, Turkey, and Cyprus surprise you? Explain.

____

____

Name _________________________ Class _________________________ Date ___________

Connect to myStory:
Bilal Looks Forward

(1) Do you identify with a specific ethnic group? Why or why not?

____

____

____

(2) List four facts about the Kurds that you learned from reading Bilal's story.

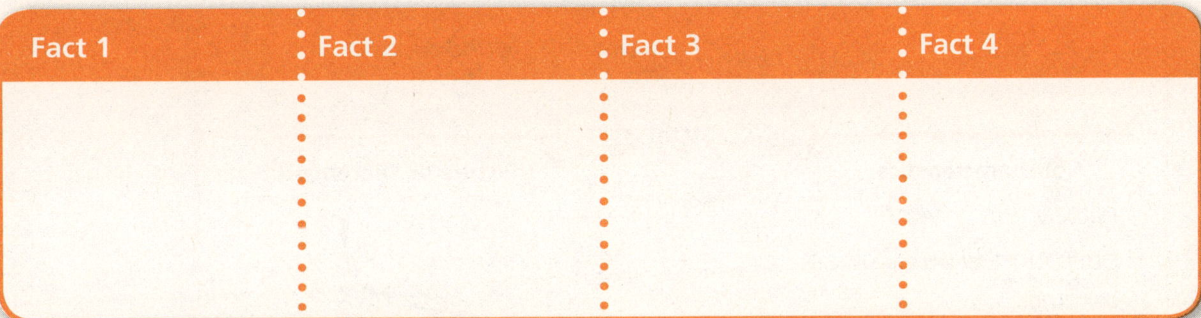

(3) How do your career goals compare to Bilal's?

____

____

____

(4) What does Bilal's story tell you about life in Turkey today?

____

____

____

Name _________________________________ Class _____________________ Date ____________

Word Wise

Word Map Follow the model below to make a word map. The key term *strait* is in the center oval. Write the definition in your own words at the upper left. In the upper right, list Characteristics, which means words or phrases that relate to the term. At the lower left list Noncharacteristics, which means words and phrases that would not be associated with it. In the lower right, draw a picture of the key term or use it in a sentence.

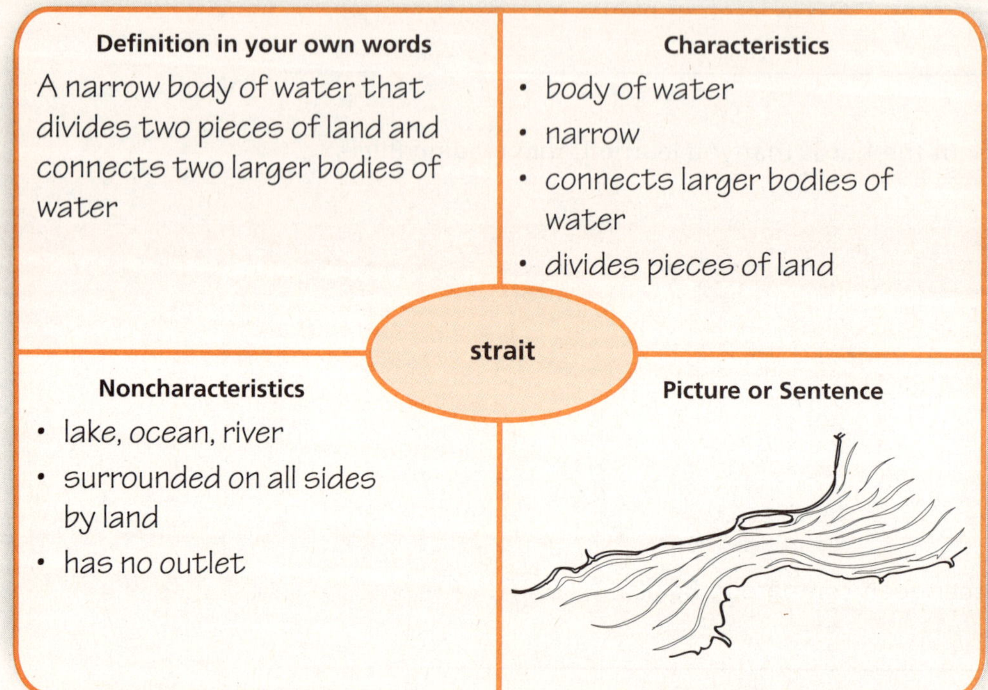

Now use the word map below to explore the meaning of the word *shamal*. You may use your student text, a dictionary, and/or a thesaurus to complete each of the four sections.

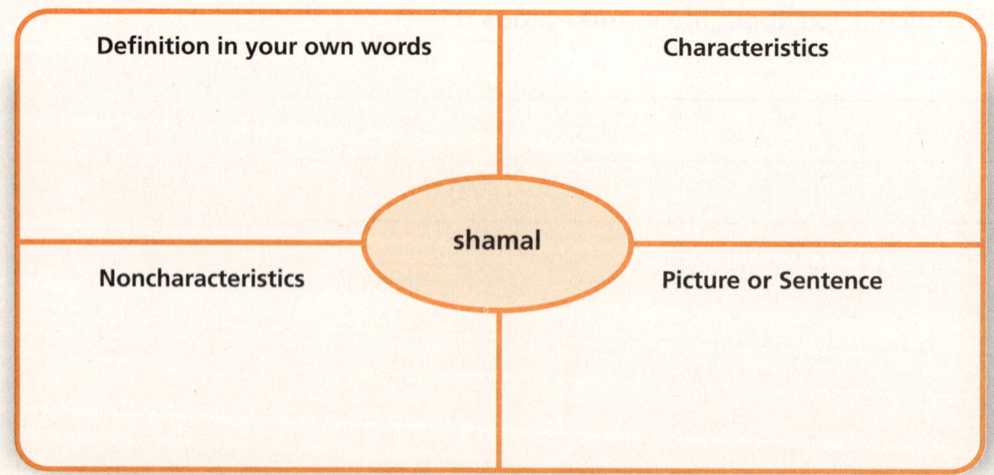

Make word maps of your own on a separate piece of paper for these words: *qanat* and *Zoroastrianism*.

Name _________________________ Class _____________________ Date ____________

Take Notes

Map Skills Use the maps in your book to make a key and to label the Places
to Know on the outline map below.

Places to Know!

Physical Features	Cities	Countries
Black Sea	Nicosia	Turkey
Zagros Mountains	Istanbul	Iran
Taurus Mountains	Tehran	Cyprus
Anatolian Plateau		

KEY

0   200 mi
0   200 km
Lambert Conformal Conic Projection

Essential Question

**What political issues have arisen from the ethnic diversity of these
countries?**

____

____

____

Word Wise

Sentence Builder Complete the sentences using the information you learned in this section. Include terminal punctuation.

1. Persian emperors sent **satraps** to ________________________________

   ____

2. A **shah** is similar to a king because he ________________________________

   ____

3. When people talk about the **Armenian Genocide**, they are referring to

   ____

4. People can assume that an **Ayatollah** ________________________________

   ____

5. The Ottomans used **millets** to organize ________________________________

   ____

6. Mustafa Kemal was known as **Ataturk** because ________________________________

   ____

Name _________________________________ Class _____________________ Date ___________

Take Notes

Sequence Use what you have read about the history of Iran and Turkey to complete the timeline. Next to each event that you list, write an *I* (for Iran) or a *T* (for Turkey).

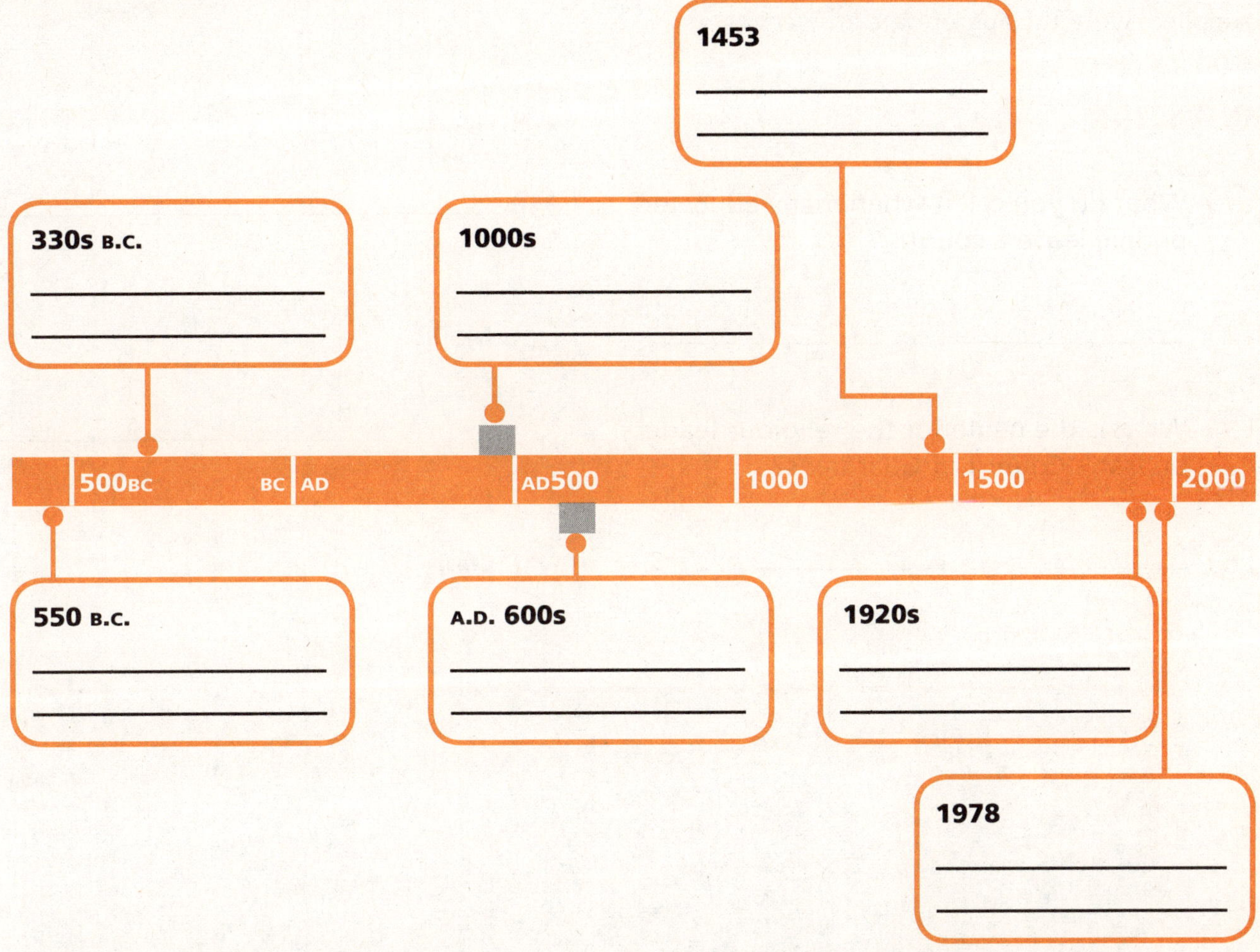

Essential Question

What role did national feeling play in the creation of modern Turkey and Iran?

____

____

____

Name ______________________ Class ____________________ Date ____________

Word Wise

Vocabulary Quiz Show Some quiz shows ask a question and expect the contestant to give the answer. In other shows, the contestant is given an answer and must supply the question. If the blank is in the question column, write the question that would result in the answer given. If the question is supplied, write the appropriate answer.

QUESTION	ANSWER
1 What do you call it when many educated people leave a country?	1 ____________________
2 ____________________	2 Majlis
3 What is the name for the religious leaders on Iran's Council of Guardians?	3 ____________________
4 ____________________	4 coup

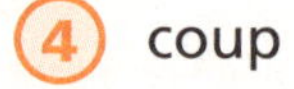

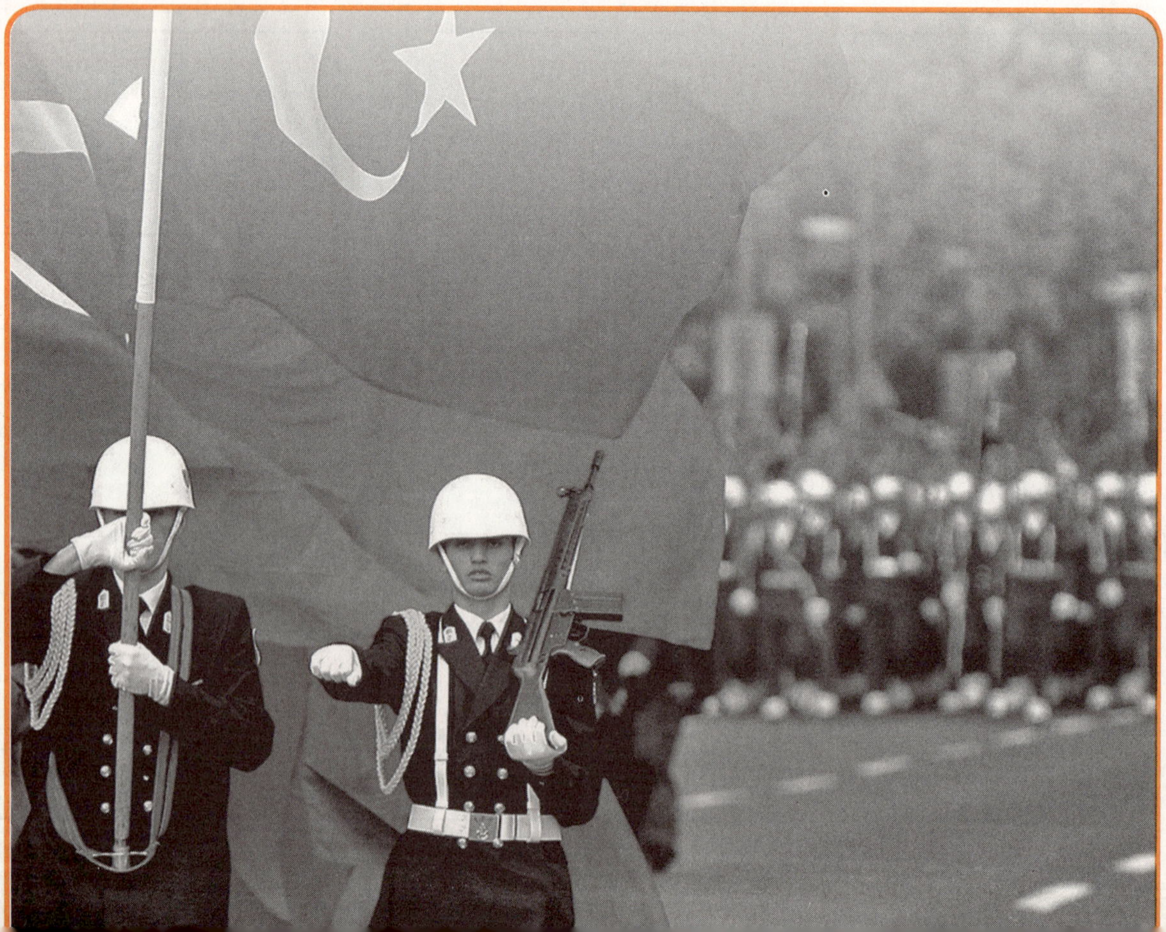

Name _______________________________ Class _____________________ Date ____________

Take Notes

Main Ideas and Details Today Iran, Turkey, and Cyprus each face major
challenges. For each issue listed, describe the main idea. Then give two
details that tell more about the main idea.

Challenges Facing Iran, Turkey, and Cyprus

Iran	Turkey	Cyprus
Citizens' Rights:	**Secular Democracy:**	**History of Division:**
Details:	Details:	Details:
Role in the World:	**Culture:**	**Events of 1974:**
Details:	Details:	Details:
Economy:	**Economy:**	**Current Situation:**
Details:	Details:	Details:

Essential Question

**What political conflict has arisen in Turkey as a result of different
views about religion?**

____

____

____

What are the challenges of diversity?

Prepare to Write

Throughout this chapter, you have explored the Essential Question in your text, journal, and On Assignment at myWorldGeography.com. Use what you've learned to write an essay describing the challenges diversity presents for one of these nations: Iran, Turkey, or Cyprus. Make sure you thoroughly describe the diversity in your chosen nation. Then, identify specific problems and clearly explain how diversity has caused or contributed to those problems.

Workshop Skill: Use the Writing Process

Writing is a bit like a board game. Sometimes you go forward a step and sometimes you have to move backwards a few steps. In the writing process, you complete four basic steps. Yet sometimes you must repeat some of them along the way.

In this lesson, you will learn about the four basic steps in writing an essay. The steps are prewriting, drafting, revising, and presenting. Each step has several parts that help you to communicate your ideas effectively.

Prewrite This step includes everything you do before you start writing. First, choose a country. Then, brainstorm about the challenges of diversity in that country. You might scan chapter headings and images or talk with a partner to get ideas. Collect ideas in note form or use a graphic organizer. Next, make an outline. It should list your main idea or thesis and at least three arguments or reasons that will explain your thesis. Return to the chapter and look for evidence—quotes, statistics, examples, etc.—that will support your reasons. Add these to your outline.

Draft Start putting your ideas into sentences and paragraphs. Follow your outline, but don't worry too much about spelling, grammar, or even complete sentences. Just get your ideas onto paper. Mark places where you may need to get more information. Think about how you can explain your ideas to readers. Try to start each paragraph with a topic sentence that communicates its main point. This will help you know what else needs to go in the paragraph.

Revise Read over your draft. Ask yourself if your ideas and explanations make sense. Think about whether "idea A" belongs before or after "idea B." Move text around until the ideas flow. Then read your draft aloud, listening for sentences that ramble on. Shorten them or create two sentences. On the other hand, if you have too many short sentences, combine sentences to keep your writing from sounding choppy. Read your essay a third time to find and fix spelling and grammar errors. While revising, you may find that you need to do more research or write more text.

Present Create a final copy of your essay. Add your name, date, and a title according to the format your teacher has requested.

Here is a simple table used for brainstorming. You may want to refer to the notes you made on page 239 for your nation.

Cyprus	
Type of Diversity	**Problem Caused**
ethnic	fighting
political	people have been displaced from their homes

Use a Graphic Organizer

Now create and complete your own graphic organizer to brainstorm ideas for your essay. You can use the table style shown above or any other style that helps you to think creatively.

Draft Your Essay

Use the graphic organizer you created to collect ideas for your essay. Then follow the steps in this workshop to draft and revise your essay on a separate piece of paper. Be sure to follow the four steps in the writing process.

What should governments do?

Preview Before you begin this chapter, think about the Essential Question. Understanding how the Essential Question connects to your life will help you understand the chapter you are about to read.

Connect to Your Life

1. Think of different ways in which the United States government of the affects your life. List at least one way in each column.

How the United States Government Affects My Life				
Laws	• Taxes	• Military	• Environment	• Transportation

Connect to the Chapter

2. Think about some of the bad times that countries go through, such as wars or economic slowdowns. In the Venn diagram below, list at least something a government should do during bad times, and something it should do during good times. In the intersection, list what a government should do at *all* times.

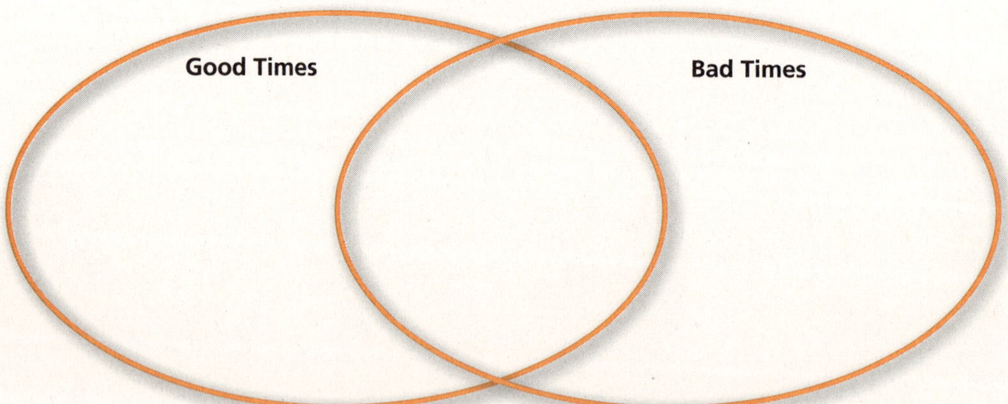

3. Preview the chapter by skimming the chapter's headings, photographs, and graphics. Using a different colored pen or pencil, add to the Venn digram some predictions of how the governments of Central Asia and the Caucasus have acted.

4. Read the chapter. Put a check mark next to your correct predictions.

Name _______________________________ Class _______________________________ Date ____________

Connect to myStory: Askar Serves His People

1 Name two problems that have affected your neighborhood or region. What caused these problems? Have they been solved?

____

____

____

2 Are the problems in your area ones that the government can solve? Explain why or why not.

____

____

____

3 What problems has Askar experienced in his neighborhood? Describe them in the table below.

Water	Electricity	Temperature	School

4 In the table above, circle the problems which you think the Kyrgyzstan government has the ability to solve.

5 How do you think these problems affect the people living in Kyrgyzstan?

____

____

____

Word Wise

Vocabulary Quiz Show Some quiz shows ask a question and expect the contestant to give the answer. In other shows, the contestant is given an answer and must supply the question. If the blank is in the question column, write the question that would result in the answer given. If the question is supplied, write the appropriate answer.

QUESTION

(1) What do you call a nation that is cut off from direct contact with the oceans?

(2) _____________________________

(3) What term describes herd animals eating so much grass that the plants cannot recover?

(4) _____________________________

(5) What do you call Kazakhstan's broad grasslands?

(6) _____________________________

ANSWER

(1) _____________________________

(2) irrigate

(3) _____________________________

(4) riot

(5) _____________________________

(6) temperate

Take Notes

Map Skills Use the maps in your book to make a key and to label the Places to Know on the outline map below.

Places to Know!

Physical Features	Countries
Caucasus Mountains	Armenia
Caspian Sea	Azerbaijan
Aral Sea	Georgia
Amu Dar'ya River	Kazakhstan
Syr Dar'ya River	Kyrgyzstan
	Uzbekistan

Essential Question

Should the governments of Tajikistan and Kyrgyzstan build hydroelectric dams if the dams will reduce the amount of water that flows to neighboring countries? Explain.

____

____

____

Word Wise

Word Map Follow the model below to make a word map. The key term *merchant* is in the center oval. Write the definition in your own words at the upper left. In the upper right, list Characteristics, which means words or phrases that relate to the term. At the lower left list Noncharacteristics, which means words and phrases that would not be associated with it. In the lower right, draw a picture of the key term or use it in a sentence.

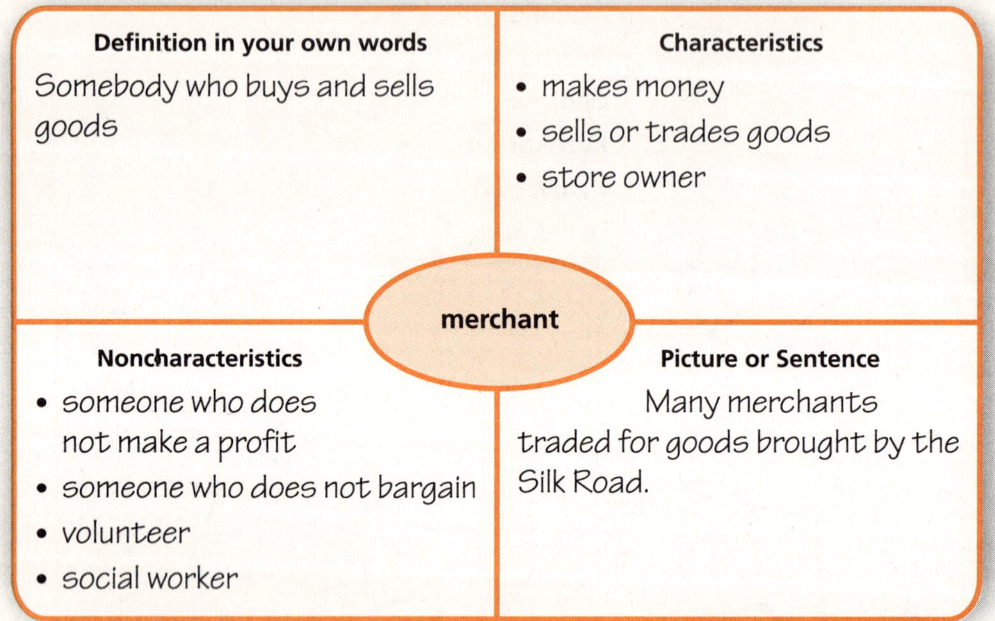

Now use the word map below to explore the meaning of the word *caravan*. You may use your student text, a dictionary, and/or a thesaurus to complete each of the four sections.

<table>
<tr><td>Definition in your own words</td><td>Characteristics</td></tr>
<tr><td colspan="2" align="center">caravan</td></tr>
<tr><td>Noncharacteristics</td><td>Picture or Sentence</td></tr>
</table>

Make word maps of your own on a separate piece of paper for these words: *sedentary, Silk Road,* and *madrassa*.

Name ___________________________ Class ___________________ Date ___________

Take Notes

Summarize Use what you have read about the history of trade and empires in Central Asia and the Caucasus to complete the concept web below. In the top section, write what you have learned about the history of trade and cultures in the region. In the bottom section, write details about the history of empires in the region.

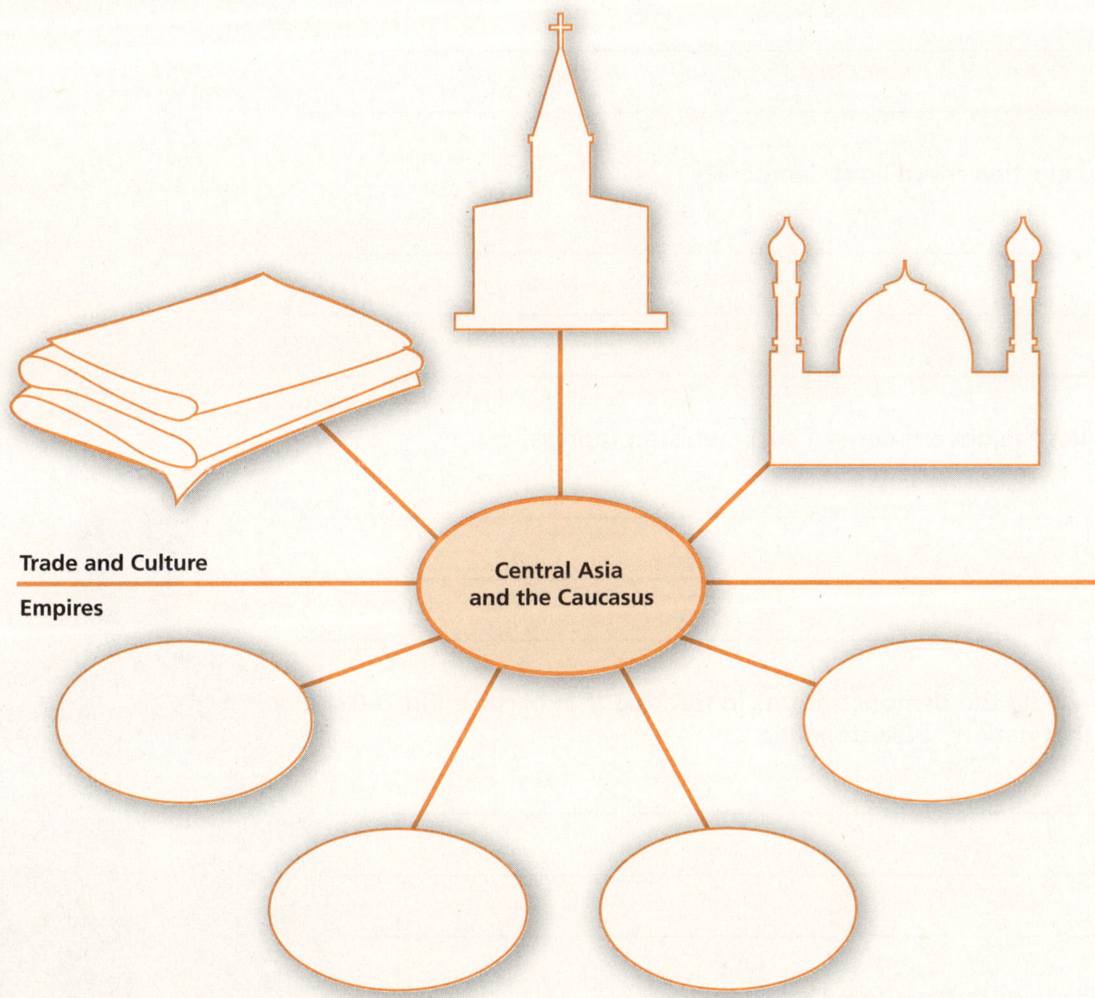

Essential Question

Why did the Soviet government encourage the Russian language in this region? Should the government choose the official language of the country?

____

____

____

Word Wise

Words In Context For each question below, write an answer that shows your understanding of the boldfaced key term.

(1) Why has the government of Kyrgyzstan supported the **akyn**?

____

____

____

(2) How does **election fraud** limit democracy?

____

____

____

(3) What makes the government of Turkmenistan **repressive**?

____

____

____

(4) What effect did the **demonstrations** in Georgia that occurred in 2003 have on that nation's government?

____

____

____

(5) What was the **Rose Revolution**?

____

____

____

Name _________________________ Class _________________________ Date ____________

Take Notes

Main Ideas and Details In the textbook, there are three headings for this section. They are listed below on the left. Write the main idea from each part in your own words. Then, for each main idea list at least two supporting details in the column on the right.

Main Ideas	Supporting Details
Cultural Life of Central Asia and the Caucasus	
Challenges for New Nations	
Building New Governments	

Essential Question

Do you think the governments of Central Asia and the Caucasus should try to make farmers and businesses reduce pollution? Explain.

____

____

____

What should governments do?

Prepare to Write

Throughout this chapter, you have explored the Essential Question in your text, journal, and On Assignment at myWorldGeography.com. Use what you've learned to write an essay about what governments should do in Central Asia and the Caucasus. Consider some of the actions governments have taken in this region. Also, think about how the role of some of these governments should change.

Workshop Skill: Outline an Essay

Good essays are not only factually correct, they also catch the reader's attention with a "hook." In addition, a well-constructed essay uses a thesis statement to prepare the reader to move through the essay.

The Hook Think about how the governments of Central Asia and the Caucasus have acted since the fall of the Soviet Union. Are there some actions you agree with? Are there some you disagree with? Find three examples. Then create a "hook," one or more sentences that will catch the reader's attention. For example, you could open with: *Imagine if your neighbor cut the water to your house so that just a trickle came from your faucet.* Notice how this statement creates personal interest in the reader. On the lines below, write some hook ideas to generate interest in the fact that how the nations of Kyrgyzstan and Tajikistan have built hydroelectric dams that have reduced the water flow into nearby nations.

____

____

The Thesis Statement After the hook, state your thesis, which is the main idea of your essay. Your thesis should state three ideas you will use to support your position. These ideas will be the focus of your three body paragraphs. In this case, the thesis statement is the last sentence in your introduction. Add two of your own ideas to the thesis statement given below.

Example *The governments of Kyrgyzstan and Tajikistan have built*

hydroelectric dams that have reduced the water flow into the nearby nations

of Uzbekistan and Turkmenistan. The action that some of the governments

of Central Asia and the Caucasus have taken concerning water shortage,

______________________, *and* ______________________ *have been controversial*

and should change.

Organize Your Essay

Paragraph 1: Introduction Remember the hook ideas? Begin your introductory paragraph with one of those and end it by clearly stating your thesis.

Paragraph 2: Body Paragraph A In your thesis, you stated three ideas about what governments should do. State one of these ideas in Body Paragraph A and use at least two details to support it.

Topic Sentence *The governments of Kyrgyzstan and Tajikistan have supported the building of hydroelectric dams.*

Detail 1 *These dams reduce the flow of water into nearby nations.*

Detail 2 ____

Concluding Sentence *To prevent a water shortage in Uzbekistan and Turkmenistan, the governments of Kyrgyzstan and Tajikistan should prohibit the building of more dams in their own countries.*

Paragraph 3: Body Paragraph B Review your thesis and note your idea for the second topic, which will be the focus of Paragraph B. Try to make a smooth transition as you begin a new paragraph.

Topic Sentence *In addition to preventing water shortages, governments in*

Central Asia and the Caucasus should also _____________________.

Detail 1 ____

Detail 2 ____

Concluding Sentence _______________________________________

Paragraph 4: Body Paragraph C Follow the steps given for body paragraphs 1 and 2 to write your third body paragraph.

Paragraph 5: Conclusion For the conclusion, summarize the ideas you presented in your thesis.

The examples of water shortage, ___________________, *and*

___________________ *shows how the roles of some of the governments of*

Central Asia and the Caucasus need to change. By studying the region's

governments, it is clear that _______________________________.

This shows that governments should _______________________

and should not ____

Draft Your Essay

Write your essay and then proofread it with a writing partner.

Essential Question

What makes a nation?

Preview Before you begin this chapter, think about the Essential Question. Understanding how the Essential Question connects to your life will help you understand the chapter you are about to read.

Connect to Your Life

(1) Think of countries that you've learned about from reading or from the news. What made each country unique and different from other countries? Write your ideas in the table below.

Things That Make Nations Different From Each Other			
Institutions	• Geography	• Culture	• Other

(2) Look at the table. Which categories do you think have the greatest effect on the individual character of a nation?

____

____

Connect to the Chapter

(3) Now think about setting up a nation from scratch. What are the basic needs of a new nation? In the concept web below, predict factors that played a part in shaping the unique nations of South Asia.

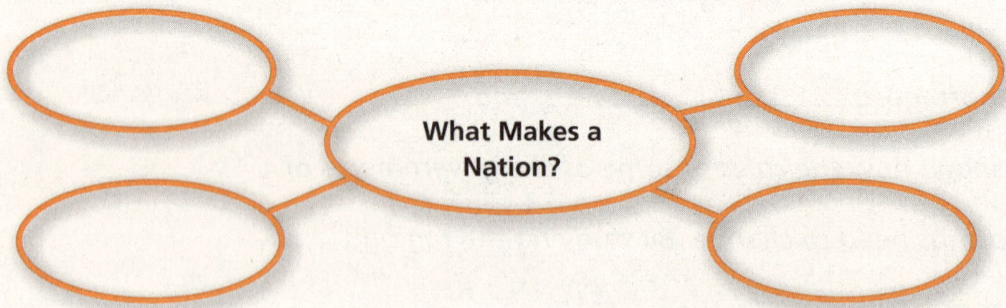

(4) After you read the chapter, return to your predictions above. Would you change any of your responses now? Why or why not?

____

____

Name ______________________________ Class ______________________________ Date ____________

Connect to myStory:
Nancy's Fruitful Loan

(1) Do you think it's important for teenagers to learn to work cooperatively with other people? Explain.

____

____

(2) What has Nancy learned about cooperation from helping her mother at the canning cooperative? Use your ideas to fill in the web below.

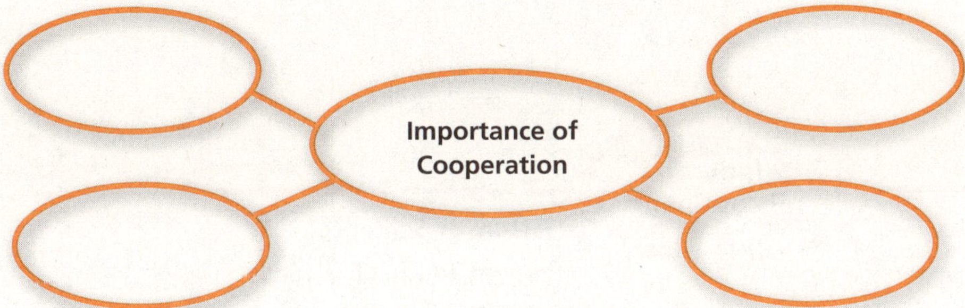

(3) How important is cooperation to the success or failure of the canning cooperative?

____

____

(4) Can cooperation help a nation to function better? How?

____

____

Word Wise

Word Map Follow the model below to make a word map. The key term *Indian subcontinent* is in the center oval. Write the definition in your own words at the upper left. In the upper right, list Characteristics, which means words or phrases that relate to the term. At the lower left, list Noncharacteristics, which means words and phrases that would not be associated with it. In the lower right, draw a picture of the key term or use it in a sentence.

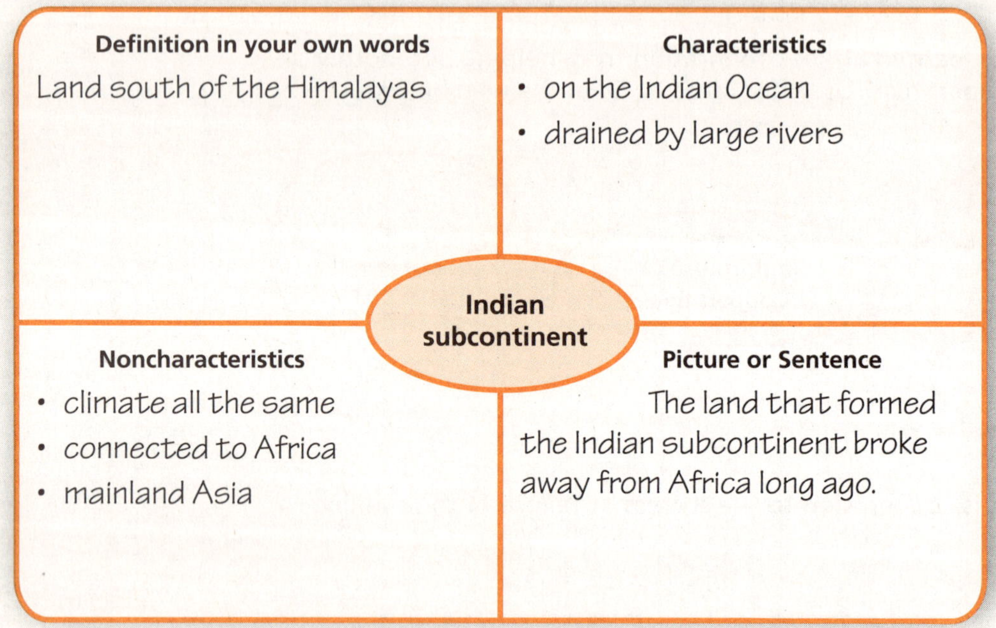

Now use the word map below to explore the meaning of the word *flood plains*. You may use your student text, a dictionary, and/or a thesaurus to complete each of the four sections.

<table>
<tr><td>Definition in your own words</td><td>Characteristics</td></tr>
<tr><td colspan="2" align="center">flood plains</td></tr>
<tr><td>Noncharacteristics</td><td>Picture or Sentence</td></tr>
</table>

Make word maps of your own on a separate piece of paper for these key terms: *Green Revolution* and *subsistence farming*.

Name _________________________________   Class _________________________   Date ___________

Take Notes

Map Skills Use the maps in your book to make a key and to label the Places
to Know on the outline map below.

Places to Know!

Physical Features		Cities	
Himalayas	Deccan Plateau	Calcutta	Lahore
Ganges River	Thar Desert	Mumbai	Delhi
Indus River	Hindu Kush		

Essential Question

**How does the geography of a nation help create a common
bond among its people and help shape its national identity?**

____

____

____

Word Wise

Crossword Puzzle The clues describe key terms from this section. Fill in the numbered *Across* boxes with the correct key terms. Then, do the same with the *Down* clues.

Across

1. The _______________________ system divides society into distinct groups.
2. a state of great understanding and freedom
3. to split a country into two nations
4. the religion that developed from the teachings of Siddhartha Gautama

Down

5. a policy in which India did not declare itself an ally of either superpower during the Cold War
6. the religion of most Indians today
7. a place where civilization begins and then spreads

Name ___________________________ Class ___________________ Date ___________

Take Notes

Cause and Effect Use what you have read about the history of South Asia to complete the table below. Give the approximate date or time period of each event. Then identify the effects of each event.

Cause	Effect
Traders carry goods from the Indus Valley civilization. **Time period:**	
Invaders enter the Indian subcontinent and mix with local communities. **Time period:**	
Ashoka takes control of South Asia after Alexander's retreat. **Date:**	
Muslim rulers establish the Delhi Sultanate. **Time period:**	
European traders set up ports. **Time period:**	
Gandhi heads a movement to force Britain to release its control over India. **Time period:**	

Essential Question

Do you agree or disagree with Gandhi's and Nehru's idea of a nation?

____

____

Word Wise

Vocabulary Quiz Show Some quiz shows ask a question and expect the contestant to give the answer. In other shows, the contestant is given an answer and must supply the question. If the blank is in the question column, write the question that would result in the answer given. If the question is supplied, write the appropriate answer.

QUESTION

1. What do you call a long poem that tells a story filled with adventure and conflict?

2. _______________________________

3. What do call you a representative government that is not based on religion?

4. _______________________________

ANSWER

1. _______________________________

2. Bollywood

3. _______________________________

4. outsourcing

Name _________________________________ Class _____________________________ Date _____________

Take Notes

Summarize Use what you have read about South Asia today to complete the table below. Write at least two important ideas that sum up each topic.

Culture

1.

2.

Population Growth

1.

2.

Pollution

1.

2.

Religious Conflict

1.

2.

Governments

1.

2.

Economies

1.

2.

Essential Question

What problems threaten the national unity of each nation in South Asia?

____

____

Prepare to Write

Throughout this chapter, you have explored the Essential Question in your text, journal, and On Assignment at myWorldGeography.com. Use what you've learned to write a essay on how the idea of a nation might differ among the nations in South Asia. Include information about South Asia's varied languages, religions, and cultures. Also keep in mind the effect of invasion and colonization on the nations' development.

Workshop Skill: Write an Introduction and Thesis Statement

Before you begin writing, review some ways to explore the Essential Question by brainstorming, free writing, or creating an idea web. Doing so will help you to figure out your thesis statement, which is the major point of your essay.

In this lesson, you will learn how to write a thesis statement and an introduction. These two parts set up your essay and provide a "road map" for your reader.

Develop a Thesis Statement Use your prewriting ideas to help you draft a thesis statement that identifies the main idea of your essay. Keep in mind that a successful essay supports and expands upon the thesis statement. All the information in your essay should connect to this important idea.

On the one hand, a thesis statement should not be too general. Ask yourself these questions: Is my thesis statement vague? Can I cover this idea in one essay, or would it take a book? For example, this thesis statement is too general: *South Asia is composed of a great variety of nations.*

On the other hand, a thesis statement should not be too specific. Ask yourself these questions: Is my thesis statement narrow? Does it focus on a very limited part of the chapter? Can I write a whole essay on this idea? For example, thesis statement is too specific: *Britain's colonial empire in South Asia affected the kind of nations that developed there.*

Here is an example of a solid thesis statement: *Many influences shaped the languages, cultures, and religions of South Asia and contributed to the kinds of nations that developed there.*

Compose an Introduction The purpose of an introduction is to present your thesis to your readers and to lead into your essay. Your introduction makes a first impression. How can you be sure that it is a good impression? Your introduction has to be interesting. It should make your reader want to read on.

Connect Start with an idea connected to your thesis: *South Asia sits at a geographic crossroads.*

Expand Develop the idea by adding a little detail: *The region is sandwiched between Europe, the Middle East, Asia, and Southeast Asia.*

Explain Let your readers know why this is important: *As a result, South Asia was a natural route and a stopping point for invaders, traders, and travelers.*

Synthesize Now put it all together: *South Asia sits at a geographic crossroads. The region is sandwiched between Europe, the Middle East, Asia, and Southeast Asia. As a result, South Asia was a natural route and a stopping point for invaders, traders, and travelers. These influences shaped the languages, cultures, and religions of South Asia and contributed to the kinds of nations that developed there.*

Write a Thesis Statement and Introduction

Now write your own thesis statement and introduction for your essay.

Thesis Statement ____

____

Connect ____

____

Expand ____

____

Explain ____

____

Synthesize ____

____

____

____

Draft Your Essay

Write your essay on your own paper using the introduction you just developed. Be sure to include three body paragraphs and a concluding paragraph. When you have finished, proofread your essay with a partner. Then write a final copy.

Essential Question

How can you measure success?

Preview Before you begin this chapter, think about the Essential Question. Understanding how the Essential Question connects to your life will help you understand the chapter you are about to read.

Connect to Your Life

1. Think of some ways to measure success in the categories shown in the table below. List at least one way to measure success to measure success in each column. For example, under school you could list grades.

Measures of Personal Success			
Family	Friends	School	Other (Sports, Arts, Chores)

2. Look at the table. Compare the ways to measure success. How are they alike? How are they different?

____

____

Connect to the Chapter

3. Now think about ways to measure a country's success. For instance, pollution levels can measure a country's success with environmental protection. Preview the chapter by skimming the chapter's headings, photographs, and graphics. In the table below, list at least one way to measure China's success in each category. Then predict if China has achieved success in each category. For example, if you think that China has high pollution, it would show a lack of success with the environment.

Measures of National Success			
Economy	Politics	Social Services	Environment

4. Read the chapter. Then circle your predictions in the table that were correct.

Name _______________________ Class _______________________ Date ___________

Connect to myStory: Xiao's Lake

(1) Name two changes you have seen in your neighborhood or region. Are these changes good or bad? Explain why.

____

____

____

(2) What changes has Xiao seen in his neighborhood or region? Write them in the table under the correct headings.

Economy	Lake Tai	Government Decisions

(3) How do you think these changes are affecting China? Write at least two predictions.

____

____

____

____

Name _________________________________ Class _______________________________ Date ____________

Word Wise

Vocabulary Quiz Show Some quiz shows ask a question and expect the
contestant to give the answer. In other shows, the contestant is given an
answer and must supply the question. If the blank is in the question column,
write the question that would result in the answer given. If the question is
supplied, write the appropriate answer.

QUESTION

(1) What do you call a person whose job is to
move with animals from place to place
during the year?

(2) _______________________________________

(3) What is the name for the major crop that
feeds most people in a region?

(4) _______________________________________

(5) What do you call the kind of land where
crops can be grown?

ANSWER

(1) _______________________________________

(2) one-child policy

(3) _______________________________________

(4) loess

(5) _______________________________________

Name _________________________ Class _________________________ Date ___________

Take Notes

Map Skills Use the maps in your book to make a key and to label the Places to Know on the outline map below.

Places to Know!

Physical Features	Countries	Cities
Huang River	Mongolia	Beijing
Chang River	Taiwan	Shanghai
North China Plain		
Plateau of Tibet		

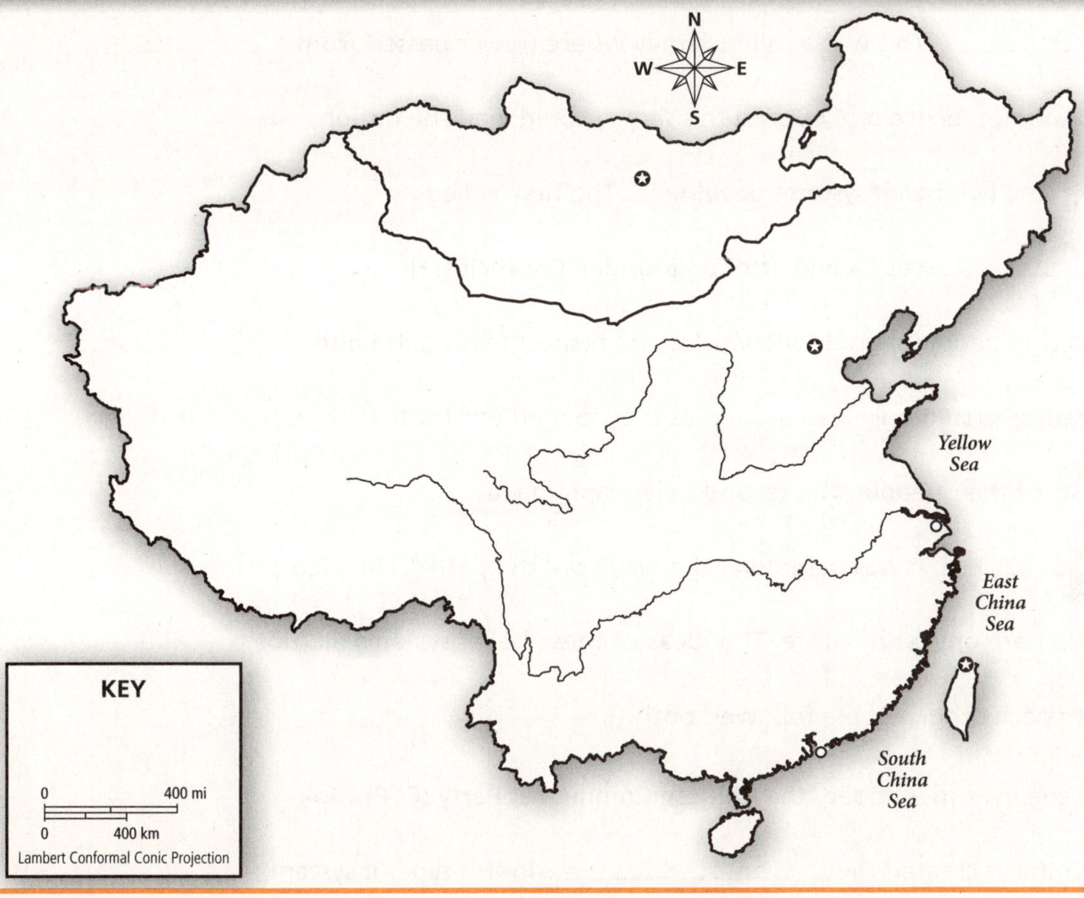

Essential Question

How can the Chinese government measure whether or not the one-child policy has been successful?

____

____

____

Word Wise

Word Bank Choose one word from the word bank to fill in each blank.
When you have finished, you will have a short summary of important ideas
from the section.

Word Bank

famine	Confucianism
Daoism	command economy
dynasty	

About 3,800 years ago, China was ruled by its first

________________________. This was a ruling family where power passed from

one person to another. No one outside this family could lead the nation.

During this time, two belief systems developed. The first, called

________________________,was named after its founder, Confucius. He

emphasized that people should follow rules and respect leaders. He also

said that leaders should only lead as long as they looked out for the

best interests of their people. The second belief system was

________________________. It was based on "the way" or "the path." The idea

was to live in harmony with nature. The ideas of these belief systems did not

conflict with each other. People followed both.

When the dynasties ended, the Chinese Communist Party (CCP) took

charge of China. It created the ________________________. In this type of system,

the government has a lot of control. It decides what crops should be grown

and what goods should be made. It assigns people to jobs. People have few

choices. The idea was that everyone would have enough to eat. But the

reality was different. The CCP made some poor decisions. This caused a

period of starvation called a ________________________.

Name ________________________________ Class ___________________ Date ____________

Take Notes

Main Idea and Details Use what you have read about the history of the region to fill in the graphic organizer below. The label above each pagoda corresponds to a heading in this section of the chapter.

Empires of China and Mongolia

Main Idea

____

____

Supporting Details

____

____

Important Ideas and Beliefs

Main Idea

____

____

Supporting Details

____

____

End of Dynasties

Main Idea

____

____

Supporting Details

____

____

China and Mongolia Under Communism

Main Idea

____

____

Supporting Details

____

____

Essential Question

Do you think the Qing dynasty was unsuccessful?

____

____

____

Name _______________________________ Class _______________________ Date __________

Word Wise

Crossword Puzzle The clues describe key terms from this section. Fill in the numbered *Across* boxes with the correct key terms. Then, do the same with the *Down* clues.

Across	Down
1. power generated by water	4. what a worker gets for doing a job
2. China's political system is a ________________________ state.	5. the average number of years a person will live
3. not able to read and write	

Name ________________________ Class ____________________ Date ____________

Take Notes

Compare and Contrast Fill in the table below to compare and contrast the politics and economies in China, Mongolia, and Taiwan.

Country	Politics	Economies
China		
Mongolia		
Taiwan		

Essential Question

What is one way that China has been successful? Give evidence from the text and from figures to support your point.

____

____

____

Essential Question   **Writer's Workshop**

How can you measure success?

Prepare to Write

Throughout this chapter, you have explored the Essential Question in your text, journal, and On Assignment at myWorldGeography.com. Use what you've learned to write an essay measuring the success of China. Include the following: the economy, politics, social services, and environment of China. Think about the amount of success achieved by China in each category, and what caused its success or lack of success in each category.

Workshop Skill: Write Body Paragraphs

Review how to outline your essay and write an introduction. Phrase the main point you want to make as a thesis statement. For example, *China has achieved great success in some areas and little success in others*. In your introduction, support your thesis with three ideas.

In this lesson, you will learn how to write the body paragraphs. Each body paragraph should develop one of the ideas you listed in the introduction that supports your thesis statement. Each body paragraph expands on the idea by giving details or evidence.

Write a Topic Sentence Start each paragraph with a topic sentence. A topic sentence must clearly state the main idea of the body paragraph, connect that idea to the essay's thesis, and provide a transition from the previous paragraph.

Support the Topic Sentence With Discussion and Facts After your topic sentence, explain and support your point with discussion and details. Discussion sentences connect and explain your main point and supporting details. Supporting details are the actual facts.

End With a Concluding Sentence Finish your paragraph with a sentence that reflects your topic sentence and pulls together the discussion and details.

Here is a sample body paragraph:

Sample topic sentence *China achieved great economic success when it changed from a command economy to a market economy.*

Supporting discussion *Since this change, China has developed one of the world's largest economies.*

Supporting detail *It stresses manufacturing, technology, and services, with agriculture remaining important.*

Supporting discussion *As the economy continues to grow, many companies have expanded and hired new workers.*

Concluding sentence *Now these companies are producing products that are exported all over the world.*

Write a Body Paragraph

Now write your own body paragraph for your essay.

Topic sentence

____

____

Supporting discussion

____

____

Supporting detail

____

____

Supporting detail

____

____

Supporting discussion

____

____

Concluding sentence

____

____

Draft Your Essay

Use the body paragraph above in your complete essay written on your own paper. Be sure that each of your body paragraphs has a topic sentence, supporting details, and a concluding sentence.

How much does geography shape a country?

Preview Before you begin this chapter, think about the Essential Question. Understanding how the Essential Question connects to your life will help you understand the chapter you are about to read.

Connect to Your Life

(1) How have the geographic elements listed in the table below affected your life? List the effects listed in each column. For example, under local weather, list the effects of precipitation or temperature on your life.

Personal Influence of Geographic Elements				
Parks, Lakes, Rivers	Local Weather	Local Crops	School Size	Recreational Activities

(2) Do you think geography has had a major impact on your life? Explain.

____

____

Connect to the Chapter

(3) Preview the chapter by skimming the chapter's heads, photographs, and graphics. In the table below, make predictions about how geographic elements affect Japan and the Koreas. For example, you might predict that South Korea's moist, hot climate enables it to grow rice.

Influences of Geographic Elements on Japan and the Koreas				
Physical Features	Climate	Natural Resources	Population	Culture

(4) After you have read the chapter, review the predictions you listed. Put a check mark next to ones that were wrong. Why were they incorrect?

____

____

____

Name _________________________ Class _________________________ Date ____________

Connect to myStory: Asuka: A Girl on the Go

① Name at least three ways in which Asuka's life is like your own.

____

____

____

② Now think about the ways in which Asuka's life is different from your own. In the table below, record at least three differences. Then circle whether these differences are better or worse. In the third column, tell why you think they are better or worse. An example is given for you.

How Asuka's Life Compares to Mine

Difference	Compares to Mine	Why?
She has two pets.	(Better) Worse	I've always wanted a pet, but my mom won't let me have one.
	Better Worse	
	Better Worse	
	Better Worse	

③ What does Asuka's story tell you about life in Japan?

____

____

____

Word Wise

Word Bank Choose one word from the word bank to fill in each blank. When you have finished, you will have a short summary of important ideas from the section.

Word Bank

foliage   scarcity

interdependent   comparative advantage

The Korean peninsula consists largely of hills and mountains. In the past, forests covered these hills and mountains. Extensive logging has reduced these forests quite a bit, which has led to mudslides in the rainy season. However, the fall months are marked, especially in North Korea, by brilliant displays of ____________________ as the leaves on the trees in the forests change color.

Because so much of the Korean peninsula consists of hills and mountains, there is a ____________________ of flat land good for farming. This shortage means that other countries with more farmland have a(n) ____________________ over the Koreas. Both Koreas must import some of their food supplies from other countries. To pay for these imports, the Koreas trade with other countries. South Korea trades an array of advanced manufactured goods with other countries. North Korea sells mostly natural resources to other countries. Such trade is an example of how the countries of the world are ____________________.

Name _________________________________ Class _____________________ Date ____________

Take Notes

Map Skills Use the maps in your book to make a key and to label the Places to Know on the outline map below.

Places to Know!

Countries

Japan
North Korea
South Korea

Cities

Tokyo
Seoul
P'yongyang

Physical Features

Mount Fuji
Honshu Island
Cheju Island
Sea of Japan
Yalu River

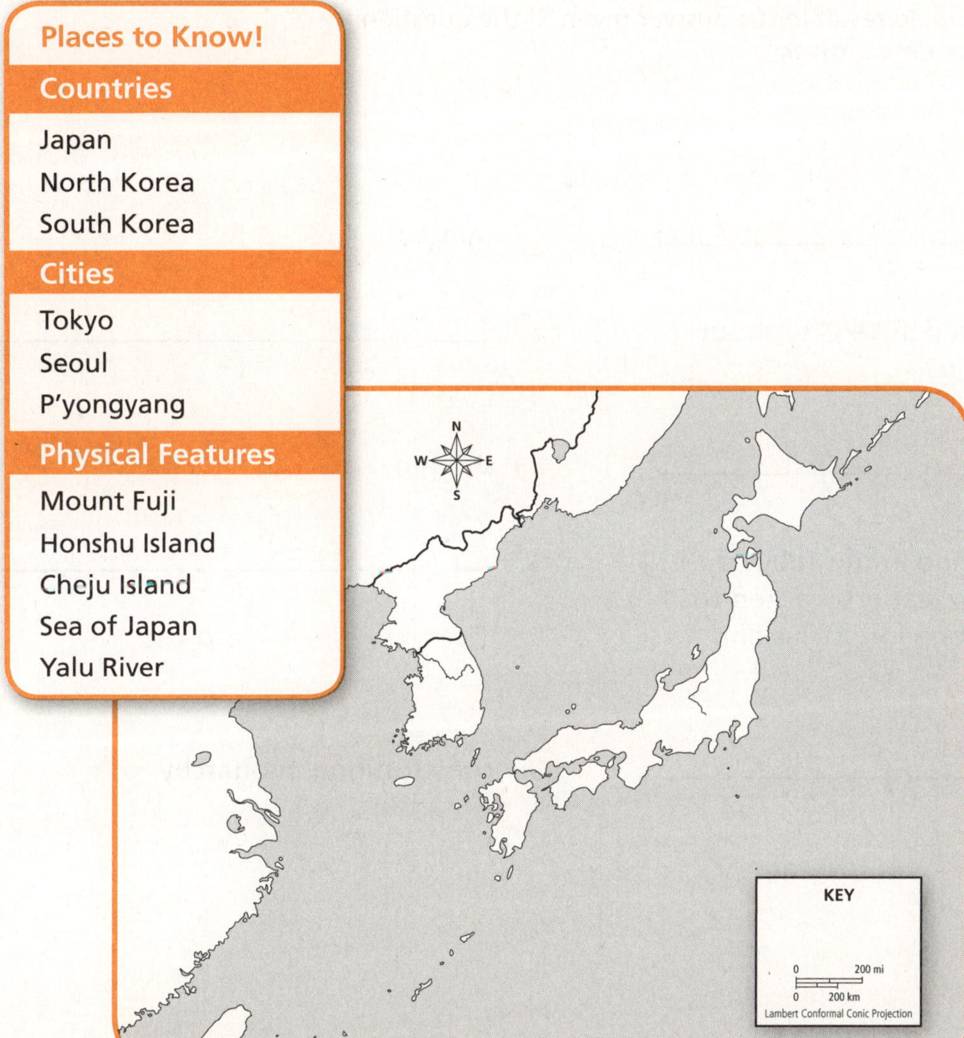

Essential Question

How does geography affect the problems that countries in this region face? What factors influence pollution in these countries?

____

____

____

____

Word Wise

Vocabulary Quiz Show Some quiz shows ask a question and expect the contestant to give the answer. In other shows, the contestant is given an answer and must supply the question. If the blank is in the question column, write the question that would result in the answer given. If the question is supplied, write the appropriate answer.

QUESTION

(1) _________________________________

(2) What conflict ended in 1953 without either side winning?

(3) _________________________________

(4) What was the period in the 1800s during which Japan's new leaders wanted to expand their nation's industries and military?

(5) _________________________________

ANSWER

(1) samurai

(2) _________________________________

(3) shogun

(4) _________________________________

(5) constitutional monarchy

Name _______________________ Class _______________________ Date ___________

Take Notes

Main Idea and Details In your textbook there are three major headings in this section. They are listed below. Write the main idea from each section in your own words. Then, write at least three supporting details for each section.

Main Idea	Supporting Details
Historical Roots	
International Conflicts and Connections	
Japan and Koreas Since World War II	

Both Japan and Korea chose to limit contact with outsiders at certain times during their histories. How do you think their geography helped them to do that?

____

____

____

Word Wise

Words In Context For each question below, write an answer that shows your understanding of the boldfaced key term.

(1) Why is South Korea's government considered a **limited government**?

____

____

____

(2) Why is North Korea's government considered an **unlimited government**?

____

____

____

(3) What makes Kim Jong-il a **dictator**?

____

____

____

(4) What were some of the effects caused by Japan's **recession** during the 1990s?

____

____

____

(5) What gods or spirits are worshiped in the **Shinto** religion?

____

____

____

Name _________________________ Class _________________________ Date ___________

Take Notes

Summarize Use what you have read about Japan and the Koreas today to fill in the table below about the economy and daily life and culture in the three countries.

	South Korea	North Korea	Japan
Economy			
Daily Life and Culture			

Essential Question

How important is geography to the differences between North Korea and South Korea?

____

____

____

How much does geography shape a country?

Prepare to Write

Throughout this chapter, you have explored the Essential Question in your text, journal, and On Assignment at myWorldGeography.com. Use what you've learned to write an essay about how geography has shaped Japan or South Korea. Consider the physical features, climate, land use, natural resources, and culture of Japan or South Korea.

Workshop Skill: Write a Conclusion

Review how to outline your essay. Then write an introduction and three body paragraphs on how geography has shaped Japan or South Korea. Be sure to include a thesis statement for the introduction and three or more supporting points in your body paragraphs.

In this lesson, you will learn more about writing the conclusion of your essay. A strong conclusion should tie together the different strands of your essay. It should give your reader the feeling that everything adds up and makes sense. First, you should restate your topic. Then, briefly summarize the points you made in the essay. After this, you should write a few sentences in which you restate your thesis in a new way. End the conclusion by pointing out the importance of the information presented in the essay.

Write a Topic Statement Start your conclusion by restating your topic. The topic statement should convey the main idea of the essay and provide a transition to your summary points. The examples given will be for North Korea.

Sample Topic Sentence: *Geography has shaped North Korea in many ways.*

Support the Topic Sentence With Summary Points After the topic sentence, write two or three sentences that summarize the main points of your body paragraphs. These sentences should not include minor details.

Summary Point *Its lack of farmland has contributed to widespread famine and the death of millions.*

Summary Point *In addition, its mountainous terrain limits the amount of living space.*

Summary Point *However, North Korea's plentiful natural resources have enabled the country to build a strong military and industrial base.*

Restate Your Thesis Next, restate your thesis statement in a way that is different from how you wrote it in the introduction. Doing this will add more emphasis to the thesis.

Sample of Thesis Restatement *As can be seen, the geography of North Korea has strongly affected the way its people live.*

End With a Concluding Sentence Finish your conclusion with a statement that stresses the importance of the information presented in the essay.

Sample Concluding Sentence *Indeed, geography has helped make North Korea the poor and dangerously unstable nation it is today.*

Write Your Conclusion

Now write your own essay's conclusion. Be sure that your conclusion has a topic sentence, summary points, a restatement of the thesis, and a concluding sentence.

Topic Sentence ____

____

Summary Point ____

____

Summary Point ____

____

Summary Point ____

____

Restate Your Thesis _____________________________________

____

Concluding Sentence _____________________________________

____

Draft Your Essay

Use the conclusion you just created in your complete five-paragraph essay written on your own piece of paper.

What are the challenges of diversity?

Preview Before you begin this chapter, think about the Essential Question. Understanding how the Essential Question connects to your life will help you understand the chapter you are about to read.

Connect to Your Life

1. Think about how there is a wide range of differences in the likes and dislikes of a group of people. For example, you may like hip-hop music while a friend prefers classic rock. Think about some general ways in which people express their differences in taste. Fill in the table below with your ideas.

Categories	Clothing	Food	Music	Interests
Expressions of Different Taste				

2. Do some differences in taste encourage or discourage interaction with other groups? Explain.

____

____

Connect to the Chapter

3. Preview the chapter by skimming the chapter's headings, photographs, and graphics. In the table below, predict the kind of challenges that diversity might present to the people of Southeast Asia. An example is given in the religious category. Fill in a prediction of your own in each of the other columns.

Diversity	Ethnic	Religious	Political	Linguistic
Challenges		When people do not share the same religion, they have may have trouble accepting each other's faith.		

4. After you read the chapter, return to this page. Circle your predictions that were accurate.

Name _______________________ Class _________________________ Date ___________

Connect to myStory:
A Minangkabau Wedding

1 How is a Minangkabau wedding similar to weddings you have attended
or seen on television? How is it different?

____

____

____

2 In the table below, list details that Ridwan's story reveals about the
Minangkabau culture.

Wedding Costumes	Food	Property Ownership

3 Think about facts from Ridwan's story. Then, write two predictions
about the cultures of Southeast Asia based on his story.

____

____

____

____

Word Wise

Vocabulary Quiz Show Some quiz shows ask a question and expect the contestant to give the answer. In other shows, the contestant is given an answer and must supply the question. If the blank is in the question column, write the question that would result in the answer given. If the question is supplied, write the appropriate answer.

QUESTION

1. What are Southeast Asia's seasonal winds called?

2. _________________________________

3. What word describes a group of islands?

4. _________________________________

5. What is the term given to a land area that is surrounded by water on three sides?

ANSWER

1. _________________________________

2. typhoon

3. _________________________________

4. tsunami

5. _________________________________

Name _______________________ Class _______________________ Date _____________

Take Notes

Map Skills Use the maps in your book to make a key and to label the Places to Know on the outline map below.

Places to Know!

Physical Features	Cities
Mekong River	Jakarta
Malay Peninsula	Manila
Irrawaddy River	Hanoi
Red River	

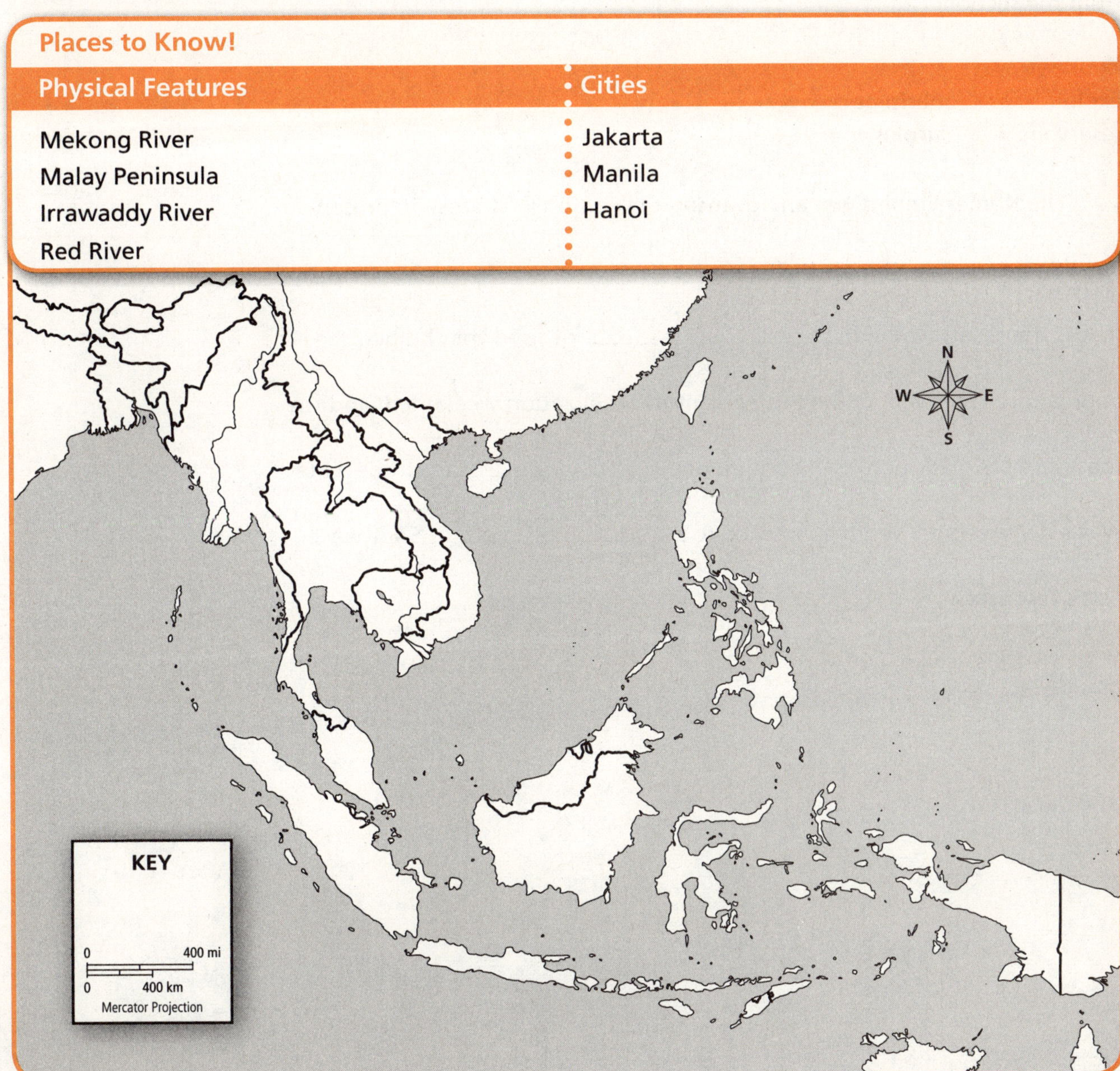

Essential Question

Why did the geography of the region help create such a diverse population?

____

____

____

Word Wise

Word Bank Choose one word from the word bank to fill in each blank. When you have finished, you will have a short summary of important ideas from the section.

Word Bank

exploit   maritime
reservoirs   surplus

The Khmer Empire was an advanced civilization that arose in present-day Cambodia. The Khmers built ___________________ to irrigate their rice fields. The result was a(n) ___________________ of food that helped the population to thrive. In time this agricultural civilization weakened, and the coastal states grew powerful because of ___________________ trade. Later, Western powers arrived that wanted to ___________________ Southeast Asia's resources.

Name _______________________ Class _______________________ Date ___________

Take Notes

Sequence Use what you have read about the history of Southeast Asia to complete the timeline below.

Timeline of Southeast Asian History

100 B.C.	Co Loa conquered by China
A.D. 600	_______________________
	_______________________
1287	_______________________
	_______________________
1414	_______________________
	_______________________
1511	_______________________
	_______________________
1954	_______________________
	_______________________

Essential Question

How did Southeast Asians react to contact with many different religions?

____

____

____

Name _______________________________ Class _______________________________ Date ____________

Word Wise

Words In Context For each question below, write an answer that shows your understanding of the boldfaced key term.

1. Why would some Indonesians prefer that their nation pursue **secular** policies?

   ____

   ____

   ____

2. What is the attitude of Myanmar's **military junta** toward dissenters like Aung San Suu Kyi?

   ____

   ____

   ____

3. Why is the Philippine government fighting **insurgency** on its islands in the south and east?

   ____

   ____

   ____

4. What does the Islamic **separatist group** of the Philippines want?

   ____

   ____

   ____

5. In what ways does **ASEAN** try to help Southeast Asia?

   ____

   ____

   ____

Name _______________________________ Class _______________________________ Date _____________

Take Notes

Main Idea and Details The topic headings in the table below match the headings in this section of your textbook. For each topic, write the overall main idea in the second column. Then, write two or three details that support the main idea in the third column.

Topic	Main Idea	Details
Southeast Asian Culture Today	Southeast Asia's position on trade routes has led to a blending of many cultures.	• Foreign merchants and immigrants arrived. • Different religious faiths came to the region and mixed with local beliefs.
Religion		
Governments and Citizens		
Population and Environment		
Diverse Economies		

Essential Question

Why has "Unity in Diversity become the motto of Indonesia?

____

____

____

What are the challenges of diversity?

Prepare to Write

Throughout this chapter, you have explored the Essential Question in your text, journal, and On Assignment at myWorldGeography.com. Use what you've learned to write an essay on the topic of the challenges of diversity in Southeast Asia. Keep in mind the region's many cultural traditions, religions, political systems, and languages. Think about how the region's geographical features attracted people from many lands. Consider, too, how Southeast Asia's history has contributed to these differences.

Workshop Skill: Revise Your Essay

Review the four steps of the writing process: (1) prewriting, (2) drafting, (3) revising, and (4) presenting. The first two steps require writing a thesis statement, an introduction, three body paragraphs, and a conclusion. Revising means carefully reading over a draft of your essay in order to correct and improve it.

In this lesson, you will learn how to revise your essay. Revision requires looking at the essay as a whole. It also involves a close look at each paragraph and sentence.

Use a Checklist Follow this checklist to revise your essay in an organized way. As you complete each task, check it off your list.

Polish Your Introduction and Thesis Statement Make sure that the opening of your essay is clear. It must catch your reader's attention.

______ My introduction is interesting and easy to understand.

______ My thesis statement is neither too general nor too specific.

Polish the Body of Your Essay and Concluding Paragraph Make sure that your paragraphs are logical and easy to follow.

______ Each paragraph has a main idea and several supporting details.

______ The transitions between paragraphs make sense.

______ My conclusion is based on information in my essay.

Polish Your Sentences Make sure that each sentence is grammatically correct and interesting.

______ Each sentence has a subject and a verb.

______ My sentences are varied. There are simple sentences, compound sentences, and complex sentences.

Proofread Each Paragraph This step requires taking a close look at each sentence and each word. Use proofreading marks instead of rewriting.

_______ My sentences are free of grammar, punctuation, and capitalization errors.

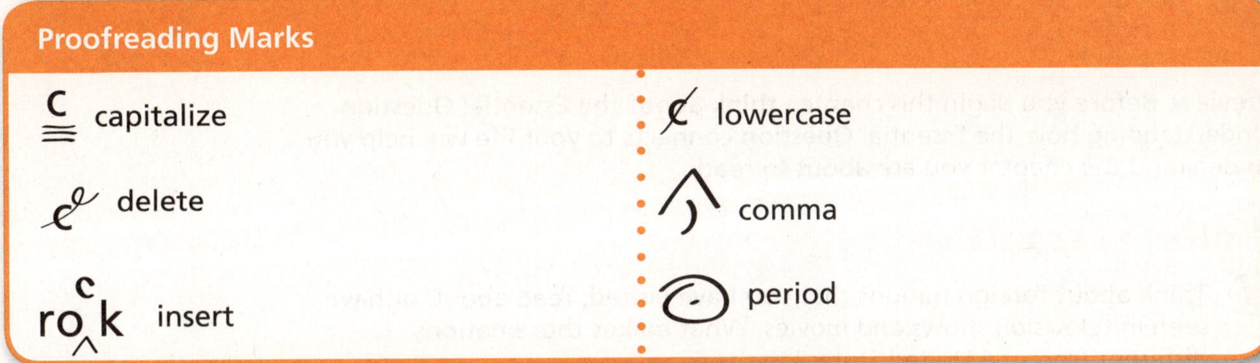

Here is a sample of a short paragraph that has been proofread. Changes have been made to increase sentence variety, too.

Diverse political systems creates different problems for the nations of southeast asia. Myanmar's military junta forbids dissent. Sometimes demonstrations erupt, and leaders like Aung San Suu Kyi get arrested. By contrast, The Philippines have a democracy with three branches of government. Nevertheless, A separatist group is rebelling against the government.

Now revise the following paragraph. Use proofreading marks to correct the errors in capitalization, punctuation, and spelling.

Religious deversity in the region sometimes leads to tension. Different forms of Buddhism spread from india and china. Islam replaced Buddhism and Hinduism in many of the region's islands. The philippines are mostly Catholic and Insurgents are fighting for a separate Islamic State there. The majority of Indonesia's mixed population is Moslem. However, the country's secular government is tolerant.

Revise Your Essay

Use the checklists in this workshop and proofreading marks to revise your own essay. Then, rewrite your final draft on a new piece of paper.

Essential Question

What makes a nation?

Preview Before you begin this chapter, think about the Essential Question. Understanding how the Essential Question connects to your life will help you understand the chapter you are about to read.

Connect to Your Life

1 Think about foreign nations that you have visited, read about, or have seen in television shows and movies. What makes those nations different from the United States?

Things That Make Nations Different From Each Other			
Institutions	• Geography	• Culture	• Other

Connect to the Chapter

2 Suppose you are going to start a new nation. What are the essential things that it would need? Before you read the chapter, flip through and note the red headings, maps, and other pictures. Record your ideas on the concept web below.

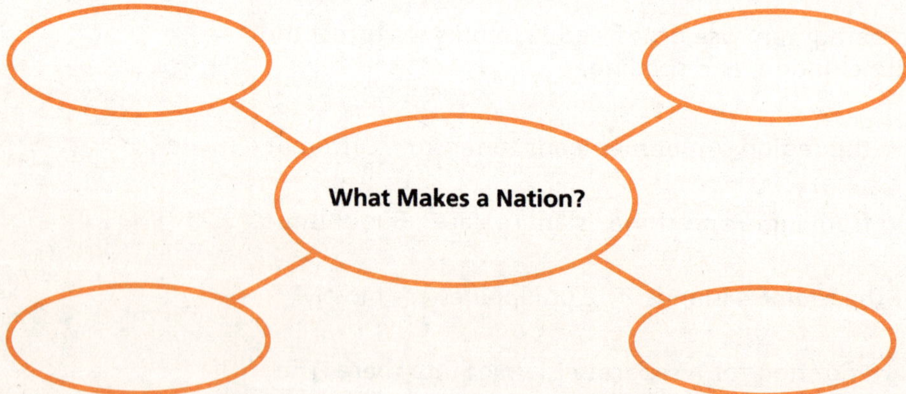

3 Read the chapter. Then connect each of the ideas you included in the web to an example from

Australia: ____________________   New Zealand: ____________________

Antarctica: ____________________   The Pacific Islands: ____________________

Name _________________________ Class _________________________ Date _____________

Connect to myStory:
Jack Connects to His Culture

1 List three customs your family follows that honors your background. Explain how these customs connect to who you are both as an individual and as a resident of the United States.

____

____

____

2 How does Jack make his Maori background an important part of his life? Fill in the table below with at least one example from each category.

Example
Language
Arts
People
Recreation
Education
Travel

3 Jack's story explains that there has been increased interest in Maori culture in recent decades. How do you think this rebirth of Maori culture connects New Zealand's past and present?

____

____

____

____

Word Wise

Vocabulary Quiz Show Some quiz shows ask a question and expect the contestant to give the answer. In other shows, the contestant is given an answer and must supply the question. If the blank is in the question column, write the question that would result in the answer given. If the question is supplied, write the appropriate answer.

QUESTION

1. What explains the way parts of Earth's crust move and shift?

2. _______________________________

3. What interior region of Australia is characterized by dry, low plains and plateaus?

4. _______________________________

ANSWER

1. _______________________________

2. atoll

3. _______________________________

4. coral reef

Name ___________________________   Class ___________________   Date ___________

Take Notes

Map Skills Use the maps in your book to make a key and to label the Places to Know on the outline map below.

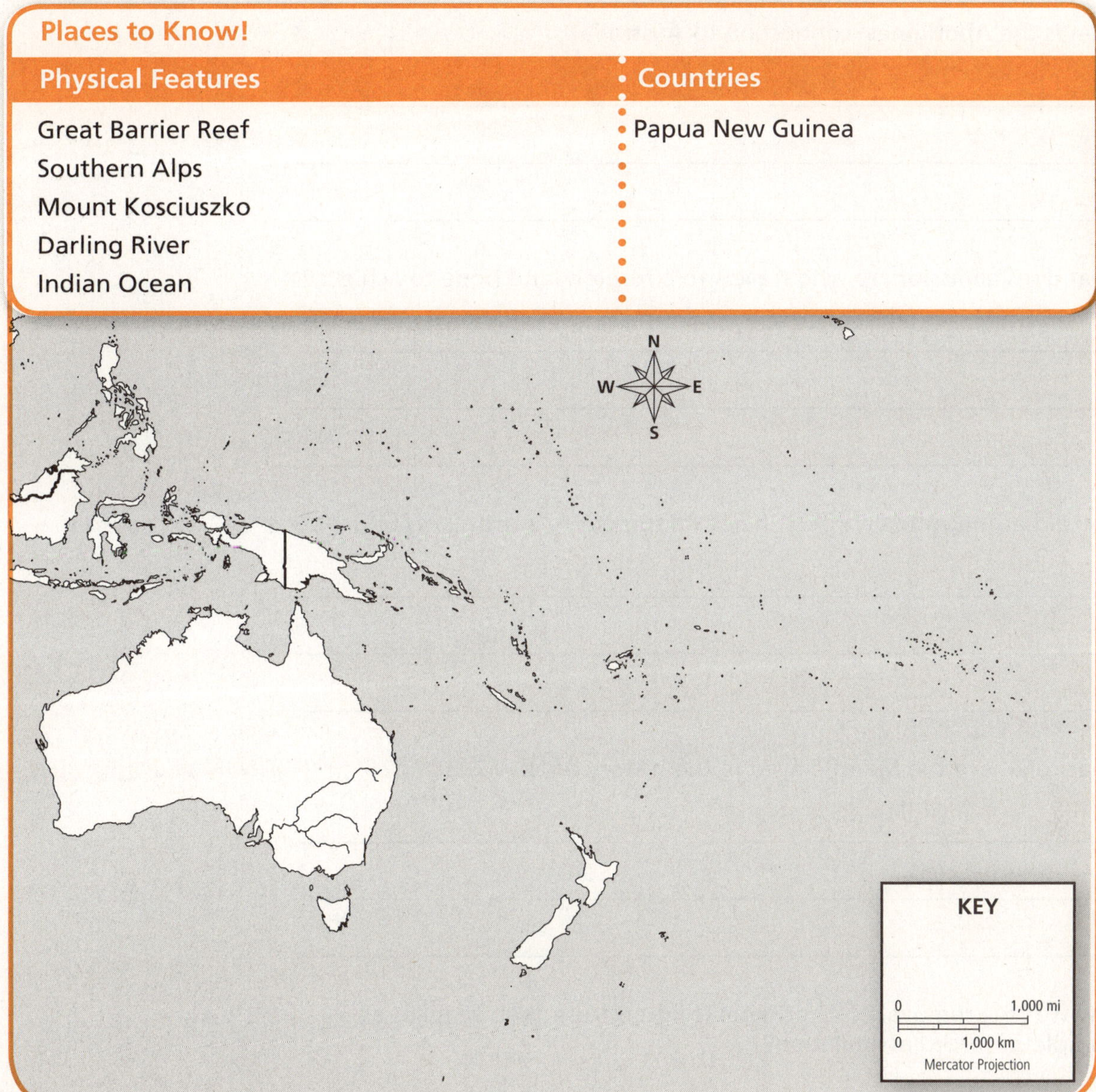

Essential Question

How have climate, location, and resources affected the development of Australia, New Zealand, and the Pacific Islands?

____

____

____

Word Wise

Words In Context For each question below, write an answer that shows your understanding of the boldfaced key term.

(1) What is the **Aborigines'** connection to Australia?

____

____

____

(2) What does a **missionary** who travels to a foreign land hope to achieve?

____

____

____

(3) How did **ethnocentrism** affect the development of Australia's culture?

____

____

____

(4) What role have the **Maori** played in the history of New Zealand?

____

____

____

(5) How was the removal of Aboriginal children from their families an example of forced **assimilation?**

____

____

____

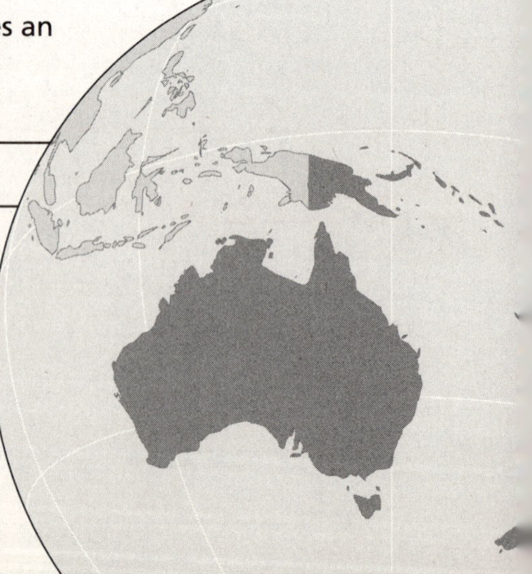

Name ________________________________ Class ____________________ Date ___________

Take Notes

Sequence The Pacific region was settled by a variety of groups. In the first box, describe the different peoples who migrated to Australia, New Zealand, and the Pacific islands. In the second box, describe the impact these people had on the region.

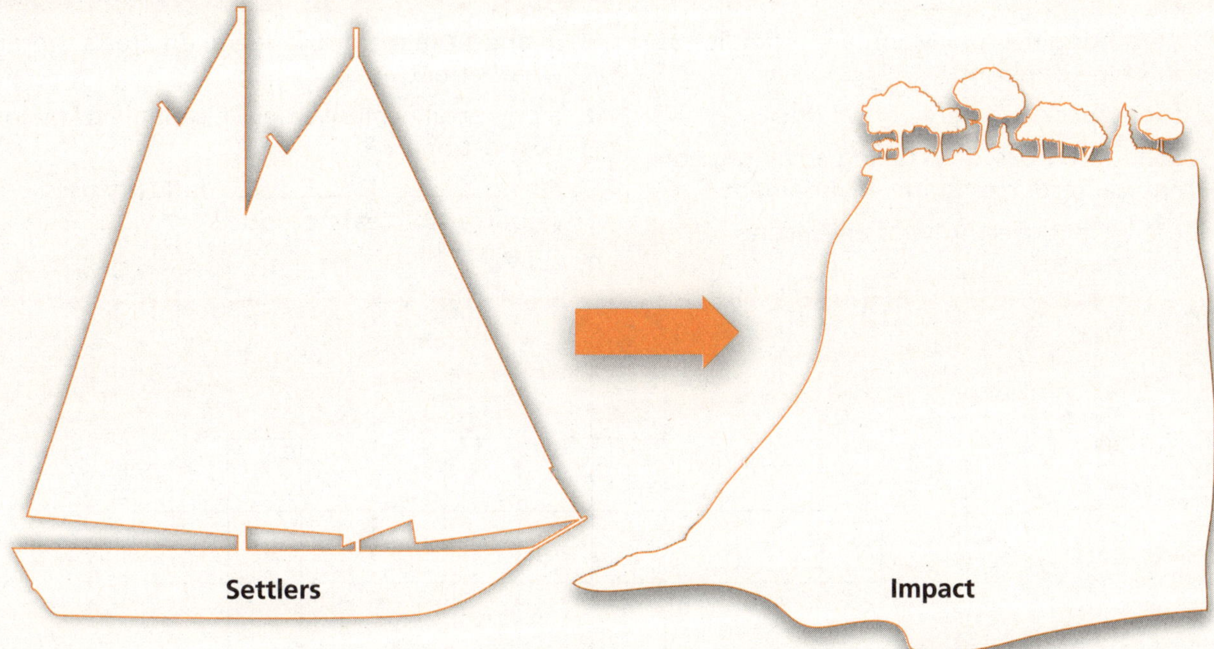

Essential Question

Does the history of colonization explain the formation of present-day nations in this region? Explain.

____

____

____

Word Wise

Crossword Puzzle The clues describe key terms from this section. Fill in the numbered *Across* boxes with the correct key terms. Then, do the same with the *Down* clues.

Across

1. the Aborigines and Maori are examples of this type of person
2. a long period of very dry weather
3. an industry based on taking advantage of natural resources in the environment
4. the violent overthrow of an existing government

Down

5. a long-term major change in an area's average weather patterns
6. a powerful explosive device capable of major destruction
7. a(n) _________________ industry uses resources to create products

Name _______________________   Class _______________________   Date ___________

Take Notes

Main Ideas and Details Use what you have read about modern Australia and the rest of the Pacific region to complete the graphic organizer. In the first box, write details about the region's people and culture. In the middle box, write details about countries' governments and economies. In the last box, write details about the region's environment.

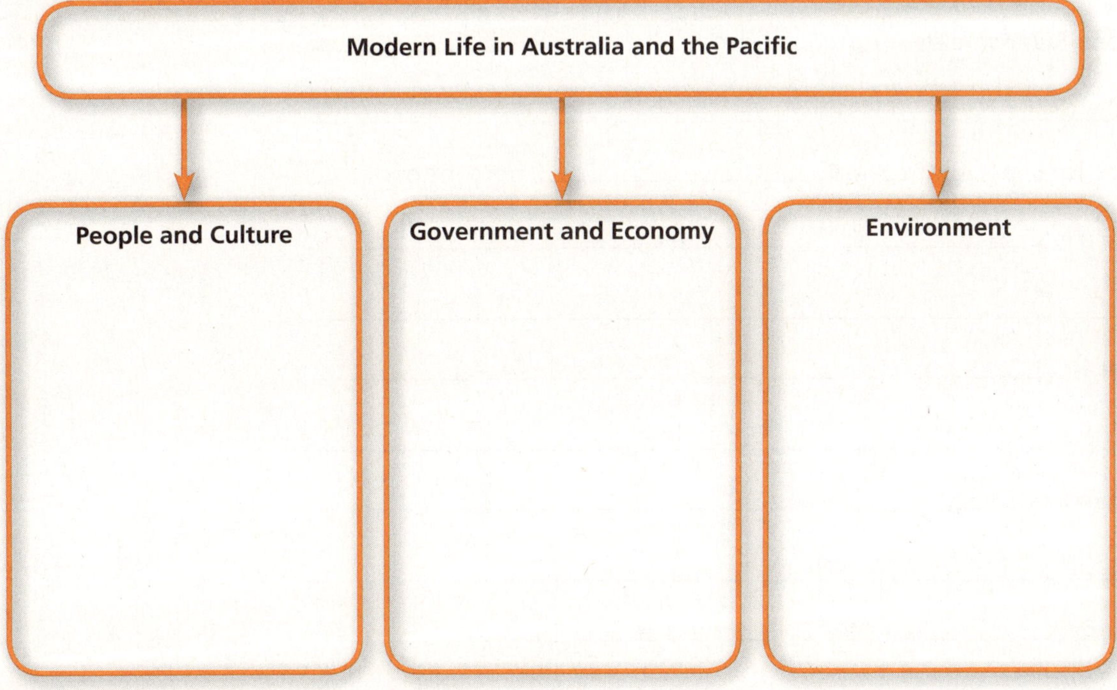

Essential Question

How do governments and economies vary among the region's nations?

____

____

____

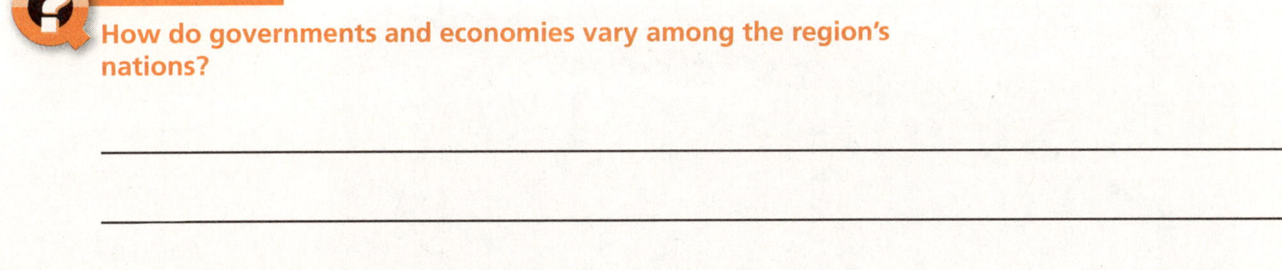

Word Wise

Sentence Builder Complete the sentences using the information you learned in this section. Include terminal punctuation.

1. **Pack ice** forms in _______________ and _______________
____

2. The **ozone layer** shields Antarctica from _______________
____

3. The thick **ice sheet** that covers _______________ percent of
Antarctica is _______________
____

4. A **glacier** is _______________
____

5. The **Antarctica Treaty** _______________
____

6. An **iceberg** is _______________
____

Name _____________________ Class _____________________ Date ___________

Take Notes

Summarize Use what you have read about Antarctica to complete the
flowchart below. In the first box, summarize Antarctica's physical geography.
In the second box, summarize Antarctica's history of exploration and
scientific research.

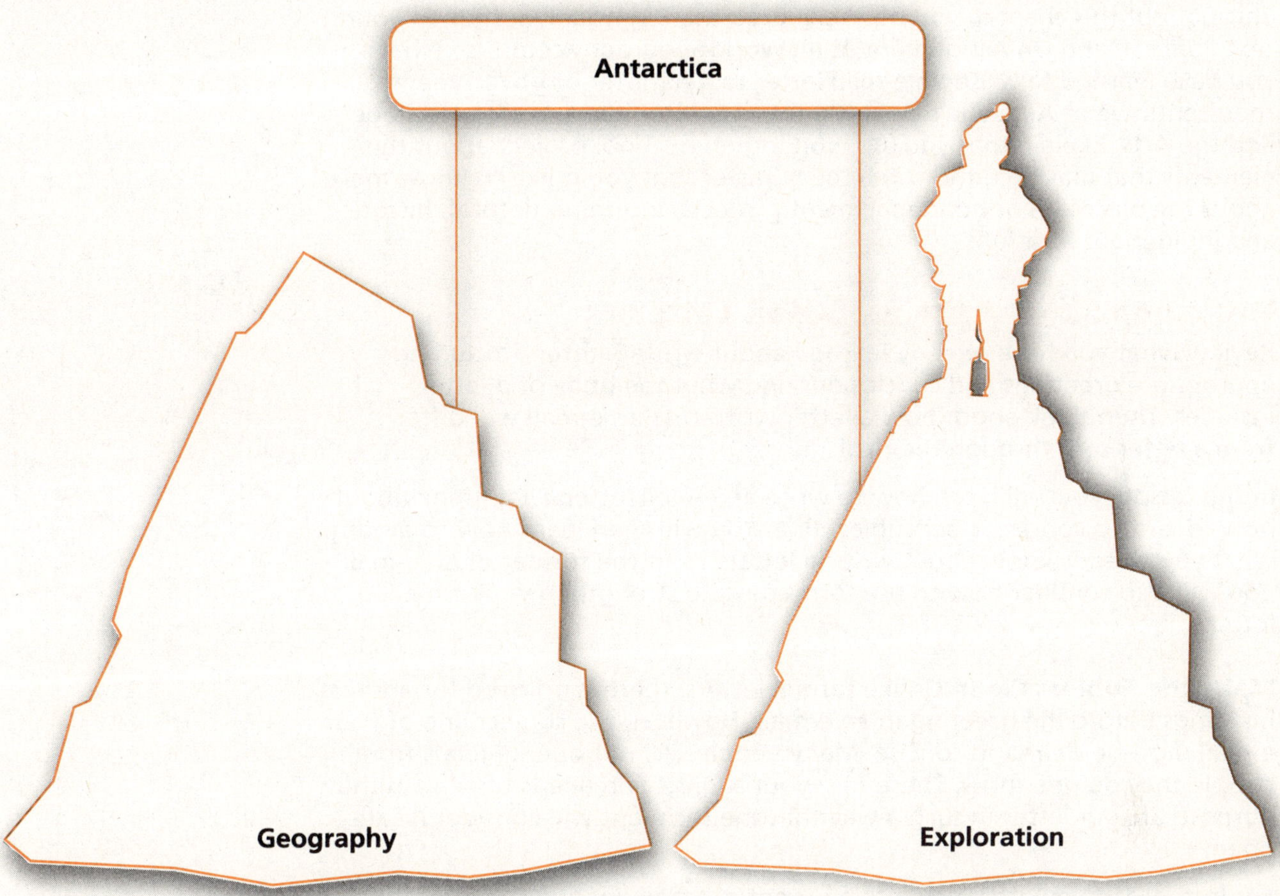

Essential Question

Why have no nations formed in Antarctica?

____

____

____

What makes a nation?

Prepare to Write

Throughout this chapter, you have explored the Essential Question in your text, journal, and On Assignment at myWorldGeography.com. Use what you have learned to write an e-mail letter to a minister or government representative at Australia's Department of Environment, Water, Heritage and the Arts. Explain that you are working on a school project about the elements that make a nation. Tell the minister that you'd like to know more about the places his or her department protects, including natural, historic, and indigenous locations.

Workshop Skill: Write an E-Mail Letter

Review what you have already learned about writing letters, including appropriate greetings and conclusions and what the body of a letter includes. Then think about how a letter written as an e-mail will differ from a letter sent through the mail.

In this lesson, you will learn how to write an e-mail letter. First, think about how to write a concise, clear subject line. You will then learn how to modify what you already know about writing letters to fit the format of an e-mail. You will also consider how to use formatting to strengthen your e-mailed letter.

Make the Subject Clear Unlike formal letters, there is no need for address headings before the greeting in an e-mail. However, the subject line of your e-mail must be clear and concise. Many people will not open e-mails from people they do not know. Therefore, your subject line needs to explain the purpose of your letter in such a way that the recipient will consider it safe to open.

For instance, if you are writing to a potential employer about a job listing, a good subject line would be *Response to ad for cashier in Saturday's newspaper.*

Write a clear, concise subject line for your e-mail to the Australian minister:

____

Get Your Point Across Quickly Like its subject line, an e-mail letter needs to be as concise as possible. Most people have more difficulty processing information in a long e-mail than in reading a long hard-copy letter. Keep your e-mail short enough that the reader scrolls as little as possible.

Plan Your Paragraphs Suppose that your e-mail to the Australian minister is three paragraphs, as described in the table below. Record the main points you want to get across in each paragraph.

Paragraph 1: Briefly introduce yourself and your project.	
Paragraph 2: Describe the kind of information you would like the minister to give you about Australia. Explain how you will use this information.	
Paragraph 3: Provide your contact information and project deadline. Thank the minister for his or her time.	

Take Advantage of Technology Think about how to use your e-mail program's features to your advantage. For example, a spell-checker is helpful. You may wish to use formatting features like boldfacing and italics to make text stand out. Don't overuse these features. Avoid emoticons and casual abbreviations. Also, do not write words in solid capitals, as many people consider that rude in an e-mail.

Now, draft the second paragraph of your e-mail using your notes above. Circle instances where you would use features of your e-mail program, such as the spell-checker or formatting features.

____

____

____

Be Ready for a Quick Reply Conclude your e-mail with appropriate thanks, complete contact information (such as your snail mail address and phone number), and your full name. There is no need to include your e-mail address since the recipient will probably just hit the reply button. The speed of e-mail means that you might receive a reply faster than you expected. Be prepared to write quick reply thanking him or her for the response.

Write Your E-mail Letter

Now use the information you jotted down in the table above to create a complete e-mail on a computer. Be sure your e-mail includes a clear subject line, a concise body, neat formatting, and a proper conclusion. E-mail it to a classmate "minister" for feedback.

Acknowledgments

Maps

XNR Productions, Inc.

Photography

2, Mike Agliolo/Corbis; 3, Saul Loeb/AFP/Getty Images; 4, L, Bill Curtsinger/National Geographic; R, Image Makers/Getty Images; 12, Jim Sugar/Corbis; 14, Indranil Mukherjee/AFP/Getty Images; 17, Wave RF/Photolibrary; 18, Galen Rowell/Corbis; 19, Jake Rajs/Getty Images; 21, Melanie Stetson Freeman/The Christian Science Monitor/Getty Images; 23, All Canada Photos/Alamy; 27, Bruno Morandi/age Fotostock; 29, SuperStock/age Fotostock; 32, ©2008 by Ira Lippke/Newscom; 33, PCL/Alamy; 35, istockphoto; 37, LB, Pearson; 38, GoGo Images Corporation/Alamy; 42, Stephane De Sakutin/AFP/Getty Images; 43, Matthew Ward/Dorling Kindersley; 45, Todd Gipstein/Corbis; 48, Kote Rodrigo/EFE/Corbis; 49, Jeff Greenberg/PhotoEdit; 51, Andy Crawford/Dorling Kindersley, Courtesy of the University Museum of Archaeology and Anthropology, Cambridge; 52, Bettmann/Corbis; 53, O. Louis Mazzatenta/National Geographic; 55, El Comercio Newspaper, Dante Piaggio/AP Images; 58, Nick Nicholls/The British Museum/Dorling Kindersley; 62, Museum of History of Sofia, Sofia, Bulgaria/Archives Charmet/Bridgeman Art Library; 64, Geoff Dann/Dorling Kindersley; 70, Philip Gatward/Dorling Kindersley; 72, Joel W. Rogers/Corbis; 74, Getty Images/De Agostini Editore Picture Library; 76, Bettmann/Corbis; 78, Bettmann/Corbis; 83, Pearson; 96, Dean Conger/Corbis; 98, Carlos Nieto/age fotostock; 103, Pearson; 104, Sovfoto/Eastfoto; 106, Charles & Josette Lenars/Corbis; 108, Iain Masterton/Alamy Images; 113, TR, Pearson; BR, Pearson; 114, George Steinmetz/Corbis; 116, Joan Pollock/Alamy; 124, SuperStock; 126, The Granger Collection, New York; 128, Pearson; 133, Pearson; 134, Franck Guiziou/Hemis/Corbis; 138, Olivier Martel/Corbis; 144, Ed Kashi/Aurora Photos; 146, Georg Gerster/Photo Researchers, Inc.; 147, The London Art Archive/Alamy; 153, Pearson; 166, The Art Archive/Dagli Orti; 168, AFP/Getty Images; 173, Pearson; 174, R, dbimages/Alamy; L, Shamil Zhumatov/Reuters; 178, Tim Brakemeier/dpa/Corbis; 183, Pearson; 188, S. Forster/Alamy; 193, Pearson; 194, Bruno Morandi/Robert Harding World; 196, Peter Gridley/Getty Images; 198, Yin Hai/epa/Corbis; 203, Pearson; 204, AP Photo/Yonhap, Yu Hyung-je; 206, dbimages/Alamy; 213, Pearson; 216, Yi Lu/Corbis; 223, Pearson; 224, George Steinmetz/Corbis; 228, Shutterstock; 229, Jonathan Marks/Corbis.